How Societies Change

Sociology for a New Century

A PINE FORGE PRESS SERIES

Edited by Charles Ragin, Wendy Griswold, and Larry Griffin

Sociology for a New Century brings the best current scholarship to today's students in a series of short texts authored by leaders of a new generation of social scientists. Each book addresses its subject from a comparative, historical, global perspective, and, in doing so, connects social science to the wider concerns of students seeking to make sense of our dramatically changing world.

- *How Societies Change* Daniel Chirot
- *Cultures and Societies in a Changing World* Wendy Griswold
- *Crime and Disrepute* John Hagan
- *Racism and the Modern World* Wilmot James
- *Gods in the Global Village* Lester Kurtz
- *Constructing Social Research* Charles C. Ragin
- *Women, Men, and Work* Barbara Reskin and Irene Padavic
- *Cities in a World Economy* Saskia Sassen

Forthcoming:

- *Social Psychology and Social Institutions* Denise and William Bielby
- *Global Transitions: Emerging Patterns of Inequality*
  York Bradshaw and Michael Wallace
- *Schools and Societies* Steven Brint
- *The Social Ecology of Natural Resources and Development*
  Stephen G. Bunker
- *Ethnic Dynamics in the Modern World* Stephen Cornell
- *The Sociology of Childhood* William A. Corsaro
- *Waves of Democracy* John Markoff
- *A Global View of Development* Philip McMichael
- *Health and Society* Bernice Pescosolido
- *Organizations in a World Economy* Walter W. Powell

How Societies Change

Daniel Chirot
University of Washington

PINE FORGE PRESS
Thousand Oaks ◆ London ◆ New Delhi

For information, address:

 Pine Forge Press
A Sage Publications Company
2455 Teller Road
Thousand Oaks, California 91320
(805) 499-4224
Internet: sdr@pfp.sagepub.com

Administrative Assistant: Chiara Huddleston
Editor: Elizabeth Magnus
Production Editor: Diane S. Foster
Designer: Lisa S. Mirski
Typesetter: Christina M. Hill
Cover: Lisa S. Mirski
Print Buyer: Anna Chin

Printed in the United States of America

97 98 10 9 8 7 6 5 4 3

Library of Congress Cataloging-in-Publication Data

Chirot, Daniel.
    How societies change / Daniel Chirot.
        p. cm. — (Sociology for a new century)
    Includes bibliographical references (pp. 135-138) and index.
    ISBN 0-8039-9017-0 (pb : acid-free paper)
    1. Social change. 2. Social evolution. I. Title. II. Series.
GN358.C45 1994
303.4—dc20   93-44572

To Helene, who has seen a lot of change

Contents

ABOUT THE AUTHOR

Daniel Chirot (Ph.D., Columbia University, 1973) is Professor of International Studies and of Sociology at the University of Washington's Henry M. Jackson School of International Studies. He was born in France. He graduated from Harvard College in 1964 and served in Africa in the Peace Corps. He is the author of other books about global social change as well as specialized works on the social history and politics of Eastern Europe. His most recent work is *Modern Tyrants: The Power and Prevalence of Evil in Our Age* (1994). This book tries to explain why in our century, despite the unparalleled degree of human prosperity and progress, so many societies have experienced destructive and awful governments.

ABOUT THE PUBLISHER

Pine Forge Press is a new educational publisher, dedicated to publishing innovative books and software throughout the social sciences. On this and any other of our publications, we welcome your comments, ideas, and suggestions. Please call or write to:

Pine Forge Press
A Sage Publications Company
2455 Teller Road
Thousand Oaks, CA 91320
(805) 499-4224
Internet: sdr@pfp.sagepub.com

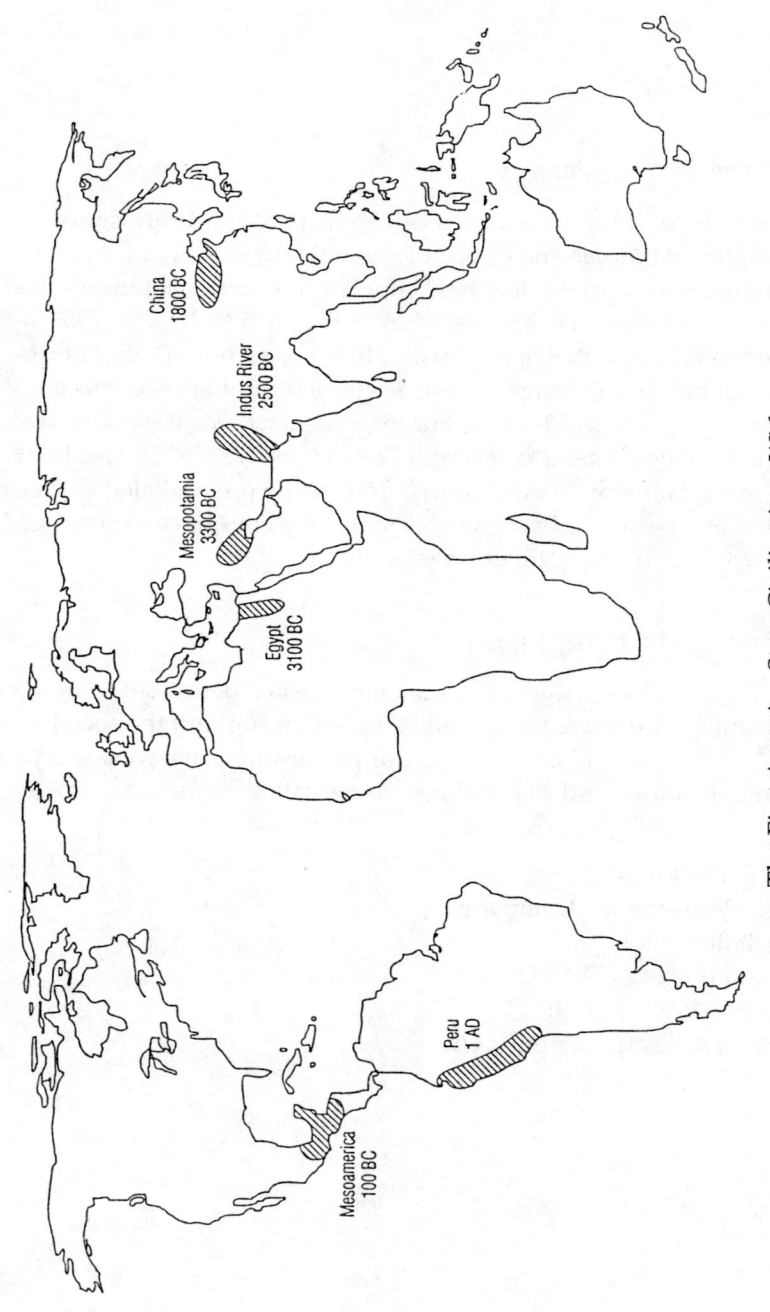

The First Agrarian State Civilizations With
Approximate Dates of Origin

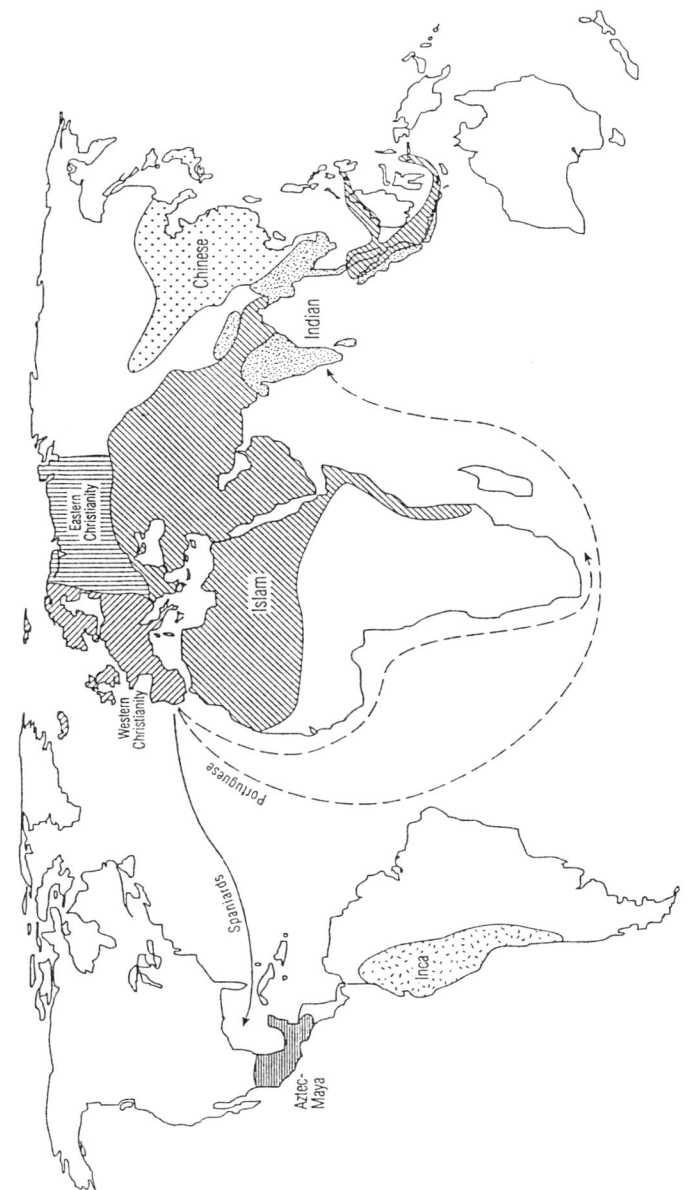

The Major Agrarian Civilizations
in About 1500 A.D.

Foreword

Sociology for a New Century offers the best of current sociological thinking for today's students. The goal of the series is to prepare students, and—in the long run—the informed public, for a world that has changed dramatically in the last three decades and one that continues to astonish.

This goal reflects important changes that have taken place in sociology. The discipline has become broader in orientation, with an ever growing interest in research that is comparative, historical, or transnational in orientation. Sociologists are less focused on "American" society as the pinnacle of human achievement and more sensitive to global processes and trends. They also have become less insulated from surrounding social forces. In the late 1970s and 1980s sociologists were so obsessed with constructing a science of society that they saw impenetrability as a sign of success. Today, there is a greater effort to connect sociology to the ongoing concerns and experiences of the informed public.

Each book in this series offers in some way a comparative, historical, transnational, or global perspective to help broaden students' vision. This volume does so very explicitly by describing how societies have changed over the past five thousand years. Responding to ecological pressures, to competition between and within societies, to demographic growth, and to the immense increase in our knowledge about how natural and social forces affect us, social structures have been altered almost beyond recognition since the invention of the earliest agrarian states. Yet, the same forces that produced change then remain present today. Some of the social forms developed to cope with repeated episodes of overcrowding, war, and inequality have failed catastrophically and produced social disasters. Others that succeeded for a time, even for a very long time, have eventually become obsolete and been overcome by further change. The search for a balance between the need to retain old and tested ways of social organization that work and finding new solutions that might be better, but that do not plunge us into unforeseen disasters remains the key problem of all societies in our industrial era as it was in the agrarian one that preceded us.

This book teaches students that even though their society is beset by difficulties that seem both new and unique, in fact many are both global and repetitions, in new forms, of challenges that have existed in the past as well. At the same time, the book is meant to show that even today we are never sure what new solutions will work, and which ones will make certain problems even worse. Though there are no final answers, the better informed an individual is about the ways in which societies change, the more likely it is that this individual will understand how to evaluate proposals for solutions to contemporary, pressing social problems.

Preface

To speak about how and why societies change is to wander into issues from the most trivial and minute to the most deeply philosophical and abstract. Why do hair styles change from one generation to the next? Why were fewer children in the United States named Robert or Mary in the 1980s than in the 1940s? Why are Japanese or French children more polite, on average, than American ones? Why did the ancient Egyptians not become monotheists like their neighbors in Israel several thousand years ago? Is the fact that Celtic speakers used to inhabit most of western and central Europe but now live only in a few fringes on the European Atlantic coastline meaningful, and if so, what does it tell us about how societies change? Does the difference between family patterns in Africa and China account for the great differences that exist between these two parts of the world?

As it happens, all of these questions, from the most profound, such as those concerning issues of religious meaning and fundamental social survival, to the most trivial, such as the one about hair styles, are of some interest. I am sorry to warn the reader that I am not going to answer any of them in this book. I do, however, hope to give the reader a useful way of thinking about such problems.

The framework for the study of social change presented in this book will be based on a few evolutionary principles. I shall emphasize the fact that societies have to adapt to changing conditions, and that some forms of change help, whereas others impede survival. By looking at the major sorts of change that have taken place over the past five thousand years since the invention of the state, I am going to illustrate the basic model with which I am working. Needless to say, this approach precludes the detailed examination of any single society.

After explaining how states and agriculture created what we have come to know as the classical civilizations, I shall spend some time show- ing why in one somewhat marginal agrarian civilization, in western Europe, there were changes so great that they transformed Europe and then the entire world, ending the agrarian age and bringing us into the industrial era.

Then I shall explore the essential features of modern industrial societies in the past two centuries that came out of that great European transformation. Although industrial societies have been a great success, they have created a set of recurring and as yet unsolved problems. These are a major impetus for further social change, and no student of how societies change can afford to ignore them.

Finally, I shall make explicit a simplified model of how societies as a whole work and how to approach the study of contemporary social change in the most useful, comparative, and historical way. I shall close by pointing out a few of the major dilemmas and paradoxes of modern society and by asking what, if anything at all, the study of social change can contribute to the resolution of our most important problems.

Throughout the book my approach is what social scientists call *macro-* as opposed to *micro-* scopic. That is, I am only looking at the ways in which big political structures, major ideas, and the most important ecological and social pressures have changed societies. To be sure, in order to discuss macroscopic change, it is necessary to have in mind certain assumptions about how individuals behave. I believe that our ordinary notions about how most people try to survive, to obtain some pleasure, to socialize, to reproduce, and to find some meaning in what they do work very well to account for why societies hold together and continue to exist. Neither basic human physiology nor psychology has changed much in this respect for tens of thousands of years.

What has changed, however, and what this book discusses is why, despite the essential psychological and biological similarity of humans today and those of, say, twenty thousand years ago, almost all aspects of our lives except for our basic physical functions are so different, and why, despite the basic similarity of all human beings on earth today (we are all one species and interbreed perfectly well) there are such huge differences in economic, social, and political behavior. I am convinced that getting a bit closer to an answer to this question is one of the main purposes of studying social change. Those with a wide range of historical and comparative facts at their command can begin to explain why there are such differences and why societies evolve in different ways. They can objectively examine what new ideas work best as societies continue to adapt and change, and this is better than relying on pure ideology or prejudice.

Traveling around the globe and across five thousand years to visit people as different from each other as twentieth-century but prestate highland warriors in New Guinea, pyramid-building ancient Egyptians,

Imperial Chinese bureaucrats from the Ming dynasty, seventeenth-century European merchants, and contemporary Americans may seem daunting. To try this in so few pages may appear foolhardy. But when all this information is connected and fitted into a comprehensible model of how and why societies change, it makes sense. Furthermore, there is no other way to begin thinking about what all human societies have in common and what distinguishes them from each other. Even for those who are interested primarily in contemporary social and political issues, it is impossible to come to intelligent conclusions without knowing what the range of social possibilities has been in the past and in what ways today's problems are the same as or different from those in the past.

This book, then, is meant to get students started in the right way to understand their society by comparing it to others, both contemporary and historical. It tries to convey the crucial fact that change is not just something that happened in the past, but that it will continue, and that it is necessary to evaluate social transformations as they occur because not all of them yield positive results. While addressing these questions, the book also seeks to broaden somewhat the knowledge that students have about the many types of human societies that have existed. I hope that this short book will make some of its readers curious and inspire them to learn more of this fascinating and important history on their own.

Acknowledgments

I thank Charles Ragin and Stephen Rutter for getting me to write this book and for their advice. I would like to express my gratitude to the Institut für die Wissenschaften vom Menschen in Vienna for having me as a visiting scholar as I was starting this project in the fall of 1992.

1

Evolution and Early Human Societies

In order to study social change it is necessary to begin with some notions about the causes and general nature of such change. This requires some comparisons between physical, genetic evolution and changes in human ideas, knowledge, and institutions. That, in turn, demands a brief perspective on events that occurred long before written history existed. Only after this will it be possible, in the second chapter, to begin with a short history of social change in the past five thousand years.

Physical and Cultural Evolution: Differences and Similarities

For at least five million years, or perhaps longer, depending on how "human being" is defined, there have been intelligent primates on earth who were evolving into the species homo sapiens. It was, however, only some forty or so thousand years ago that anatomically modern homo sapiens, humans who were physically just like us, entirely replaced older types of humanoids.

Though there continue to be scientific controversies about the origin and evolution of modern humans, the basic facts are established. We evolved from apelike creatures, probably in eastern Africa. It is thought that it was in southern or eastern Africa, somewhat over 100,000 years ago, that fully modern homo sapiens first appeared. From there we spread out to the other parts of the world. As with all living things, competition within the species for food and mates, competition from other species, and the pressures of changing climates favored those with certain physical and mental characteristics and not others.

There are no single solutions to survival. Some species—sharks or cockroaches, for example—find environments in which they can survive and reproduce for millions of years without much change. (Such environments to which organisms adapt are called *niches*.) Other species are subjected to critical challenges that kill so many that the species is extinguished, except, perhaps, for a favored few who are a little quicker or a little smarter, or who happen by pure chance to have slightly better insulation, or more offspring, or any of countless useful traits. It is in no way obvious that what we as humans consider "advanced" traits always ensure survival. Neither the sponges that inhabit the oceans nor earthworms would strike most of us as particularly interesting or clever creatures, yet they survive pretty much as their ancestors did tens or hundreds of millions of years ago, and they are wonders of biological adaptation who have occupied secure niches on earth.

Evolution is a combination of probabilities, and from our human, subjective point of view, it works in a cruel way. Those who have genetic—that is, inheritable—characteristics that are useful will, on average, survive and reproduce more successfully than others. Mutations of genes that produce inheritable differences are random and generally harmful. But some mutations turn out to be useful, and individuals who have such useful traits are more likely to pass them on to their offspring than individuals who succumb because they lack such a trait. The more intense the pressures from the environment and the greater the competition for survival, the more likely it is that rapid evolutionary change will occur.

Evolutionary biologists used to think that evolution was a fairly smooth, continuous process. More recent evidence suggests it is not. For example, it is now thought that dinosaurs, which were, in our terms, the most advanced life form on earth for tens of millions of years, died out fairly quickly some sixty million years ago because of a catastrophic change in the earth's environment, due, perhaps, to the earth's collision with large objects from space or to a sudden rise in volcanic activity, either of which would have raised so much dust in the air as to cool the earth and change the climate. There have been other such periods of colossal and fairly sudden mass extinctions of plants and animals in the past, and these were followed by periods of very rapid (that is, rapid in geological terms) evolutionary change.

The extinction of dinosaurs opened the way for birds, who are probably the direct descendants of some of the dinosaurs, and for mammals, who evolved from earlier reptiles, to flourish. It is not that dinosaurs were poorly adapted to their earth, but that their earth changed. It is not that mammals were more clever, bigger, stronger, or faster, but that they were smaller and less reliant on the kinds of food destroyed by the ecological catastrophe that killed the dinosaurs.

Survival and evolution are not functions of virtue or of anything human beings can recognize as an inevitable march toward some kind of perfect being. There is no guarantee that in the future humans will survive longer than certain insects or microscopic creatures. We may not. The most adaptable and secure form of life may not turn out to be us.

It was the recognition of this startling and ultimately terribly frightening fact that made Charles Darwin's writings instantly controversial after the 1859 publication of *On the Origin of Species by Means of Natural Selection or the Preservation of Favored Races in the Struggle for Life.* Just as earlier the Copernican revolution in astronomy, which proved that the earth turned around the sun and was therefore not at the center of the universe, was deeply disturbing to humans, so was Darwin's discovery of how evolution worked. People want to feel that they are the most important part of the universe, grander and more meaningful than cockroaches, apes, or ferns.

For all of recorded human history, which only goes back some five thousand years, and perhaps long before that, humans have thought of themselves as vastly superior to all other creatures. In historical times elaborate theologies were worked out claiming that we were favored by the supernatural lords of the universe whose special children and objects of attention we were. If there is a single fact that distinguishes the modern age from the past, it is this awful awareness that we are mortal as a species, not just as individuals, and that we have no special protection from the forces of nature. Most people do not accept this even today, but the knowledge is available and it takes ever greater capacities for denial to refuse its implications.

Nevertheless, modern humans do have some special traits that distinguish them from all other species of animals. At some time our distant ancestors acquired the ability to communicate and store knowledge and so pass it on to their offspring. Clearly other mammals, birds, and perhaps even some other animals can do this to some extent. But their ability to store knowledge and pass it on is limited, whereas humans' ability to do this continues to expand and no limit is in sight. The ability to teach young how to survive gives them an advantage they would not otherwise have. The ability to learn new technologies and pass them on, and the consequent continual increase in humans' ability to manipulate the natural environment, has made us what we are today: the dangerous masters of the world, able to perform miracles, but also capable of destroying much of the earth.

At least since the time that fully modern humans have existed, cultural evolution has changed the ways in which humans live far more than physical evolution. There is no reason to doubt that physical evolution continues, but it takes many generations for even small changes to become noticeable. There is no evidence that physical evolution takes place any more quickly now than in the distant past, and as far as humans are concerned, significant evolutionary changes take place over tens of thousands, even hundreds of thousands of years. Compared to this, the speed of cultural change is almost incomparably greater, and it continues to accelerate. Our ancestors who died in, say, 1890 would not believe their eyes if they were resurrected and placed in O'Hare Airport in Chicago. But then, few young people in 1940 could have imagined that in their lifetimes technology or social mores would change so much, and not many of us alive today can confidently predict how our great grandchildren will live.

Culture, in the sense being used here, refers simply to the store of knowledge any society possesses. It might be considered analogous to the genetic code carried in our cells that determines our physical structure. The ideas that make up a culture contain the "codes" or "blueprints" according to which societies perform their economic activities, make decisions, and organize their interactions among themselves. Cultures also encompass the means of communication: languages, arts, and ways of expressing feelings that people use with each other. Finally, it is within cultures that we find the thoughts that people have about the meaning of their lives as well as interpretations of the social and physical universe in which we all live. There is no way of knowing whether any other animals speculate about why they live and die, or about the meaning of the universe. We do know that all human societies spend a great deal of time thinking about such problems, and some of the answers they come up with have a strong influence on their social institutions. This is the part of culture that helps us decide how satisfactory or unsatisfactory our lives may be, and thus what we would like to change.

From this it is quite clear that any comparison of cultures to genetic codes is merely an analogy. Genes do not sit around wondering why they exist, and they are not able to change themselves by will. Even though cultures are sometimes surprisingly resistant to change and are in no case infinitely plastic, they do respond to changing circumstances and discontent. Even within a single lifetime people can learn new ways. Yet the analogy between genetic and cultural evolution is worth keeping in mind, because similar pressures cause both. It is just that the process and rate of change are vastly different.

This is a cumbersome way of stating the obvious. Humans can learn from their experience, but genes cannot. We are conscious of our cultural memories, of our knowledge, and we can choose to use or discard what we know.

This is not to deny that our understanding of our experiences is often so poor that changes in cultures, and in what is passed on or not, are practically as random as the ways in which genetic mutations and evolution occur. Thus it is only by hindsight that we can tell what cultural changes turned out to be adaptive or maladaptive in the past, and current debates about how we should adapt show that we may not be all that much wiser about how to conduct change than our ancestors. In actual practice, cultural evolution works in as cruel and random a way as physical evolution. There are survivors and failures, and for individuals in those cultures that fail, the price may range from gentle absorption into other cultures to very severe suffering and widespread premature death.

Cultural change (which is just a broader way of saying social change) was not always as rapid as it is today. It used to be that most people lived pretty much the way their parents had lived. For example, from the time of the great pyramids in Egypt, built forty-seven hundred years ago, to the time of Cleopatra, a bit over two thousand years ago, the pace of change was so slow that few people in Egypt were aware of it. During that time there were significant advances in metallurgy, agriculture, ship building, astronomy, mathematics, statecraft, historiography, and much more. But most Egyptian peasants in the Nile valley and delta were largely ignorant of these changes; for them life continued much as it was hundreds, even thousands of years before.

In the past five hundred years, however, and especially in the last two hundred, technologies, social organizations, and cultures started to change so quickly that ordinary individuals in the most rapidly changing countries began to perceive how this was taking place in their own lifetimes. Now it is commonplace to think that change can be measured in decades rather than centuries or millennia, and there are hardly any people left in the world who do not know this.

Some indication of the increasing rate of social change can be gauged by looking at the numbers of people alive at any one time and the speed of population growth. Up to the fifth millennium B.C. (between 5000 B.C. and 4000 B.C.) it probably took at least fifteen thousand years for the human population to triple. There were no more than about five to seven million human beings alive just before agrarian societies were invented in the fourth millennium B.C. Then because of this invention the population started to increase much faster, reaching between one hundred and fifty and two hundred million at about the time of Christ. This means, very roughly, that it tripled every fifteen hundred years. The rate of growth after that seems to have slowed a bit. By the year 1500 there were some four hundred million humans. But then a new era began, and with it a whole set of rapid changes that allowed population growth to accelerate again. In the twentieth century the population has more than tripled in less than one hundred years. Although no one believes that this rate of increase can continue much longer, what has happened to population obviously reflects major social and technological changes: control of many epidemic diseases, huge increases in our capacity to grow and transport food, and great increases in our general level of well-being. Despite all the images we have of starvation and human tragedy in the world today, almost all of it is caused by political problems rather than by our inability to provide enough for ourselves. The average standard of living of human beings is much higher than in the past, and this is what has allowed us to live longer and reproduce more successfully.

The growth of population can also serve as a shorthand way of reminding us that human social change does not occur in isolation. It has an effect on the environment and may, in the long run, prove to be highly dysfunctional for the survival of the species, as well as destructive of many forms of plant and nonhuman animal life. Increasing population pressure may cause some societies to lower their birth rates, as has already happened. Will it be those societies that reproduce at a lower rate who will turn out to survive best, in marked contrast to most of human history when those who reproduced most had the best chance of long-term survival? Can some societies thrive while others do not? Will population pressure destroy humanity and much of the earth? Will there be adaptation to this new threat, as there has been cultural adaptation to past problems of human survival? The truth of the matter is that taking a problem like population size shows how all aspects of social change are related and how these are in turn related to other forms of life on earth and to the earth's future in general. It also shows how difficult it is to come to final answers about the meaning and long-term consequences of change, or to be certain about the direction in which we ought to change in order to survive better. And now, as before, the risks of maladaptive cultural change are substantial: Serious mistakes can be as fatal now as they were in the past, but on an even larger scale.

This fact has very serious implications that few of us are willing to recognize. It means that certain social habits and institutions to which we are attached may be harmful in the long run, even if they were beneficial in the past. Some changes that we might wish to make could produce more harm than good, and others that we may not like may be necessary, so that societies who make them are more likely to be successful. As in the case of biological traits, vast numbers of social institutions are neither clearly positive nor clearly negative in this respect. But we can never be perfectly sure when certain traits will turn out to be dysfunctional because of changing circumstances, or when forms of behavior that were once considered undesirable will turn out to have great positive value. In a sense, with social institutions as with biological traits, the only sure way to know what really works and is most adaptable is to look at the past. The future remains cloudy.

An example of a social habit that may turn out to be highly functional is the tendency of people who are better off in the modern world to have fewer children than those who are poorer. This is a reversal of very ancient biological patterns in which more successful individuals tended to reproduce more and thus to perpetuate whatever genes they had that contributed to their success. But in a changing environment where overpopulation may be a serious problem, it is conceivable that those societies that are more successful in producing wealth and comfort for their people are also behaving in more functional ways to ensure their long-range survival by reproducing less. Or perhaps not. Perhaps those who overcrowd the earth now will actually inherit it. Those who are having fewer children may be engaging in behavior beneficial for the human race but detrimental to their direct descendants and cultures. No one knows yet. Nor do individuals think in such terms when they make their own decisions about whether to have more children.

We think we are intelligent, conscious, and calculating beings. Indeed we are just that when it comes to individual behavior in the context of our own social systems for which we understand the rules of behavior and the consequences of our actions. But when it comes to larger issues of what is functional or dysfunctional in the process of social and cultural evolution, our knowledge is often far too limited for us to calculate, though this does not prevent our leaders, our philosophers, and our ideologues from trying. True as this is today, it was even truer in the past when humans had far more limited knowledge about how social systems worked or failed.

Causes of Change in Early Societies

The pressures felt by early human societies can be deduced from archaeological evidence, from analogies with other types of life, and from the data gathered by anthropologists in the nineteenth and twentieth centuries about those few societies that still lived in technologically primitive conditions.

In an ideal environment the human population tends to grow, and eventually, unless there is migration or a rise in death rates, overcrowding occurs. Modern homo sapiens have never had much to fear from predators, though no doubt the occasional unlucky human got eaten by a lion. Nor have vegetarian animals been dangerous competitors. Not even microscopic disease-bearing forms of life have ever presented a major threat to humans as a whole. Humans are so intelligent and so adaptable that they have been able to occupy a wide variety of geographical niches, drawing food from so many sources that they could occupy a very wide range of habitats. Humans adapted to environments from the tropics to the Arctic, from very wet to very dry climates, and from lowlands to high altitudes long before the invention of writing or even agriculture.

But geography and particularly climate are not constant over time. Parts of the world once covered by glaciers became warmer and then again colder, deserts turned into lush forests and dried again, oceans rose and sank, creating new land bridges or islands. Such changes could be temporary, as when there were unexpected years of drought, or more long lasting, as when glaciers advanced and withdrew in cycles lasting thousands of years in the Northern Hemisphere to change the climate of whole continents. The combination of overcrowding and climatic changes put great stress on human societies. We know that even without it, in many places humans wiped out large game by overhunting and found themselves short of food.

Whatever the causes, where there had been adequate resources— enough animals to hunt, or fish to catch, or wild cereals and fruit to pick—there would suddenly not be enough. In premodern times, and especially in preliterate ones, making the necessary technological changes to adapt to sudden crowding caused by population growth, changes in climate, overuse of resources, or a combination of all three was a slow process. It took generations to adapt, so to survive some people had to move to other places or die. Increased competition for resources or the arrival of migrants from less favored places caused inevitable conflicts over scarce resources, so that pressure from the environment, whatever its causes, was always likely to produce fighting. Some human groups were exterminated, others were triumphal. Some migrated, others did not. Some developed habits so ideally suited to their environment that they multiplied quickly. Others, less lucky or living in places subjected to more uncertain climates, multiplied more slowly or died out. In any case, we know from bones found that few humans lived much beyond the age of thirty and that most of those born never lived beyond childhood.

The notion that at some distant time in the past humans lived in a kind of Eden, a near paradise with no conflict or stress, in tune with their environment, is an illogical fantasy entirely inconsistent with what we know. It was invented in historical times, in places where overcrowding had led to deep social divisions between rich and poor, between the few with power and the many without it, when life had become even harder than before. The idea that somehow long ago, before recorded history, we were all at peace with our environment and ourselves has persisted into modern times and become the basis for many religious and political ideologies. However attractive some of these may be, it is worth remembering that they are wishful thinking. After all, if this had been the case for all human societies in the past, they would not have changed very much. Perhaps some were happier than others, had an easier time with their environment, faced few predatory human migrants, and learned to control their birth rate so that they did not overcrowd their land. They stagnated while societies stimulated by greater pressures adapted, changed, and eventually spread because of their technological and social advances. Eventually, the happier few who existed in balance with their environment were overrun by the anxious many who had developed stronger cultures in order to cope with the challenges presented by their environment.

From Collecting, Hunting, and Fishing to Agriculture

One of the most important technological changes in human societies, the one that prepared the way for the evolution of modern societies, was the slow shift away from gathering, hunting, and fishing toward agriculture, that is, the domestication of food plants. There is considerable evidence that agriculture was invented in several different places, using different crops: wild wheat in the Near East, rice in Southeast Asia, maize in America.

Probably what happened was that in some fairly lush environments with abundant edible wild crops the human population grew too large to be sustained by existing resources. Desiccation related to the global retreat of glaciers at the end of the last ice age some ten thousand years ago may have contributed to pressures on the population, particularly in the Near East, where people were forced into fertile but suddenly overcrowded river valleys. The same phenomenon occurred in the highlands of Mexico and perhaps in the Yellow River valley of northern China and the Indus valley in what is now Pakistan. Whatever the causes, people who had to live from crops and could not fish or hunt enough to supplement their diets began to sow and cultivate the wild grains they were used to eating in order to increase production. This allowed population densities to grow much faster, and crowding in such places increased even more.

Even before this, some people had been able to live in fairly compact settlements on shores rich in fish or shellfish. But it was agriculture and its eventual spread from a few centers of innovation that radically transformed human societies by allowing very high population densities.

The settlement of people into compact villages and the occasional small town and their transformation into agriculturists brought about enormous social changes. For one thing, it became possible to accumulate a surplus, to store cultivated grain from year to year if the crop was good. The almost simultaneous domestication of some animals for meat, milk, and hides also meant that there came to be a number of productive goods that could be accumulated, exchanged, or stolen. Before that, territories and resources could be fought over, but there were few if any goods to seize and accumulate as such.

The availability of surpluses to steal, combined with a vast increase in population density and consequent rapid overcrowding, once again, in the most advanced societies, especially in those restricted to valleys surrounded by more hostile environments, created the potential for frequent wars. Disputes over control of land and resources, of goods, became far more common. Flight for those who lost such battles became more difficult than when small human bands wandered about as collectors, hunters, and fishermen, so resistance against aggression became more crucial.

We know that the incidence of warfare went up dramatically with the invention of agriculture. This meant, of course, that some individuals who were particularly good at fighting gained privileged positions, as did others who were skilled at mediating disputes between competitors within a village or between villages. It also meant that some strong and skillful individuals could start to accumulate surpluses, personal wealth, to use to enhance their positions. It was especially men with greater physical strength, the ability to convince others to follow them, and skill at war who could accumulate more possessions and gain prestige as well as wealth. Land, domesticated animals, and wives could be fought over, raided for, or exchanged. Unequal distribution of these valued possessions fueled more conflict.

In the highlands of New Guinea there survived stone age people at exactly this stage of development, with no knowledge of metallurgy, well into the middle of the twentieth century. They practiced agriculture with digging sticks (the technical term, strictly speaking, is *horticulturist*, with the term *agriculturist* reserved for those who learned to use animal-drawn plows) and lived in settled villages sharing confined and isolated mountain valleys. When these highlanders were visited by anthropologists from the outside, they were found to live in a state of almost permanent war. The wars were not usually very deadly because one or two deaths would bring temporary truces, but raids, killings, rapes, kidnappings, and organized looting parties were common, and from time to time, fairly sizable massacres could occur.

Horticulturists in the Amazon jungle, most notably the well-studied Yanomamö, were also found to live in conflict-ridden societies. This could be attributed to the strains placed on them by population pressure. When villages grew too big, fights erupted that forced one part to emigrate and look for new lands.

The few gathering, hunting, and wandering fishing people who survived into modern times and were studied by anthropologists, ranging from far northern Eskimos (Inuits) to the Kalahari !Kung, were found to be much more peaceful. They lived in very small bands, had little or no surplus to steal, and tended to evade competition from others by moving away. It is not that they were any gentler by "nature," but that their circumstances predisposed them less to war. When faced by competitors who already practiced agriculture or horticulture, they had little choice other than fleeing into ever more remote areas because their numbers and technological levels did not permit them to resist successfully.

We will see in the next chapter that the combination of agriculture, increased population density, and the resulting great increase in social conflict within and between groups led directly to the single most critical innovation in human organization ever undertaken, the invention of the state. For the time being, however, it suffices to say that this sketchy description of how agriculture began and what its consequences were allows us to draw an important conclusion about the nature of early social change. The causes of that change were complex and stretched out more than several thousand years. In the Near East, sedentary agriculture began about ten thousand years ago, and the first states appeared five thousand or so years later. Change occurred because of ecological pressures, that is, the interaction between geographic change and the ways in which humans themselves altered their environment by reproducing themselves, migrating, and adapting products available to them. Growing crops changed the environment as cultivated fields replaced wild grasslands, forests, and swamps; humans learned to further adapt geography by such techniques as irrigation; population size changed and put new and greater pressures on resources; and humans altered their behavior to adapt. It was all part of a long chain of causes and effects, and it would be difficult to untangle one from the other. Each change produced adaptations and changes that became the causes of further change.

We are obviously very far from the days when humans first began to cultivate crops. But it would be quite wrong to think that it is only in modern times that we have had the power to alter our ecological environment. On the contrary, even before agriculture humans could overfish and overhunt, wiping out whole species of edible animals, and thus force migrations to occur. But with the invention of agriculture, ecological degradation, overcutting of trees, silting of rivers, and destruction of wildlife began to occur at a much faster pace than before. Irrigation in semiarid or arid zones produced soil salination. What we now experience as pressures put on our resources because of overpopulation and overuse of the land is an old phenomenon, as is the attendant human conflict that may result from this.

Reference Notes
(Full references are in the bibliography)

To obtain a detailed understanding of evolutionary biology would require more reading than most nonspecialists would care to pursue. However, the various collections of essays by Stephen J. Gould, for example, *Hen's Teeth and Horse's Toes*, provide an excellent introduction to the topic. Howard Kaye's *The Social Meaning of Modern Biology* explains how advances in biology have been interpreted by social analysts and how they have shaped social theorizing. Carl Degler's monumental *In Search of Human Nature* traces the revival of Darwinian thought in social science after a long period of eclipse.

Among the anthropologists who have used an evolutionary approach to understand broad social change and written highly readable books are Walter Goldschmidt (*Man's Way*) and Marvin Harris (*Cannibals and Kings*). Harris in particular stresses the importance of ecology and the interaction between human societies and geography, with an emphasis on how social change modifies the natural environment and how that forces further adaptive changes on societies.

The collection edited by Brian Spooner, *Population Growth*, contains some of the most illuminating articles ever written about the connection between demography, the invention of agriculture, and the development of the state. As important is Ester Boserup's *Population and Technological Change*. General population figures for the distant past have been estimated by archaeologists and anthropologists. Colin McEvedy and Richard Jones report some consensus figures about human populations throughout the world in their *Atlas of World Population History*.

2

Agrarian Societies

The invention of agriculture about ten thousand years ago was the key technological development that shaped historical societies, those that most humans lived in until the nineteenth century. But it was the invention of the state in about 3000 B.C. that was the key social invention that determined how historical societies would be organized.

If cultures can be thought of as a set of codes that contain the knowledge as well as the hopes and fears of humans about their environment and as a whole set of blueprints for how to build social systems, then social systems themselves should be seen as the actual institutions that organize human activity. They never work as perfectly as the cultural codes demand, but it is from their successes and failures that cultures receive the information necessary to modify their codes.

The family is obviously a most ancient social organization, determined in large part by biological imperatives. Though there are different types of families, the small group that consists of several adult male-fathers, several female-mothers, children, and the occasional elderly grandparent who has survived is the most basic human social unit that existed long before modern homo sapiens. For most humans, there was never much choice. The family was the only way for people to be able to regularly and easily satisfy their sexual urges, to procreate, and to have the companionship most humans crave in order to give their lives meaning. The small band made up of closely related individuals was the best and most lasting way to establish the cooperative arrangements between people without which humans cannot survive. Almost no individual is able to obtain enough food or security to survive long alone. That is invariably true for small children, and almost as true for adults.

But the family and the small band made up of a few related small families do not provide sufficient structure to conduct life in densely populated agrarian societies (that is, those practicing agriculture to obtain most of their food). We know from the study of gatherers and hunters such as the Australian Aborigines that long before the invention of agriculture small bands maintained links with others and wove elaborate bonds of intermarriage, kinship, and mutual dependence with each other. But such relations were intensified and put under extreme pressure by the crowding that resulted from the sedentarization of human populations. We have already seen that this resulted in a much higher incidence of warfare and the development of rudimentary forms of stratification, in which a few individuals, primarily males, gained greater wealth and prestige because of their abilities as warriors, leaders, or mediators.

With further growth of population, especially in areas constricted by deserts or mountains that made escape to other fertile regions difficult, these pressures, conflicts, and increasing social differentiation led to the formation of states, the most powerful human organization yet devised.

The Invention of the State

There is, of course, no way to be certain of how the first states were formed. But again, using archaeology and anthropologists' studies of recent prestate societies, we can get a pretty good idea of what probably happened.

Two kinds of individuals gained increasing prominence in the unusually fertile, constricted valleys where agriculture had begun because of changing climates. These were mediators who could resolve disputes about control of land and resources and war leaders who could help their group force favorable solutions to conflicts on their neighbors.

From very early prehistorical times, certainly as long as there have been modern homo sapiens and probably even earlier, in the time of Neanderthals, some individuals seemed especially gifted as healers and as interpreters of natural phenomena. Such individuals could also explain the seemingly vast array of supernatural, magical forces at work in the world. Such people are often labeled *shamans* by anthropologists. They were often looked to as leaders, mediators, and advisers. It was natural for people to assume that talent as shamans and many associated skills might be passed on by heredity, so that even in prestate societies certain families had prestigious reputations as healers, interpreters of the supernatural, and advisers.

With the increased intensity of conflict between sedentary villages practicing agriculture, those with the skills of shamans came to be in even greater demand. They could cast spells to ward off enemies, they understood the supernatural forces that had to be propitiated in order to obtain good harvests or strength in war, and they knew how to handle people to organize them and get them to cooperate. Being a successful shaman, in fact, requires great social skill. It involves convincing people that one has access to great mysteries and magical powers. Unless we happen to believe in the particular supernatural forces at work, we can easily see that it is not such forces that are actually manipulated by shamans, but the beliefs of those around them. To be sure, some people long ago learned about the value of certain plants as medicines, and as more technological skills were developed, some craftsmen learned the secrets of making better tools. But magic and the appeal to the supernatural, the ability to convince or soothe or induce awe—these were and to a considerable extent remain more persuasive than mere technological knowledge.

Shamans, or what we might today call priests, were the first specialists freed from regularly producing for themselves, because they collected payment for their services. They were the first specialized profession to exist in human societies.

Making war is also largely though not entirely a social skill. Brute strength, good reflexes, training—all the skills that make great athletes also make good warriors, too, especially when war consists of close hand-to-hand combat and direct, physical confrontation, as it did until very recently in human history. But the ability to combine such athletic skills with leadership and tactical foresight turns the adept killer-warrior into a leader, just as it turns the superior athlete into a team leader rather than just a great individual performer.

Growing conflict in human societies put a premium on the skills of war leaders and shaman-priests. Professional soldiers probably became the second oldest profession. If a single individual managed to combine the talents of both, then he was likely to become a great leader.

There is a vast difference between being a leader in a prestate society and a state society. In the former case, even if some skills and prestige could be passed on to one's descendants, leadership was essentially a matter of performance. The individual with the rare combination of skills could achieve influence, wealth, and even power, that is, the ability to command others. But when such a leader died, his wealth and power would be dissipated. And until leadership was institutionalized, not even the most powerful leader could be sure of being obeyed in a moment of crisis, much less after the crisis had passed.

When Europeans first ran into nonstate peoples they completely failed to understand what was going on. In the Americas the advanced civilizations, such as the Aztecs and Incas, had social structures the Europeans understood very well when they arrived in the sixteenth century because they were so similar to their own, with kings, nobles, commoners, peasants who were virtual serfs, slaves, and so on. But in large parts of North America, particularly in the plains and the far West, which Europeans invaded later and where states did not yet exist, they mistook temporary war leaders or great shamans for kings and were surprised when agreements they came to with such individuals turned out to be nonbinding or quite unenforceable.

The same thing happened in Africa, where there were great states with kings and hereditary nobles, but where there were also nonstate peoples with impermanent leadership. In Nigeria, for example, which the British conquered in the late nineteenth century, the British quickly came to an agreement with the Fulani-Hausa Empire and city states in the north, which had typical political and social structures for advanced agrarian societies. But the Ibo in southeastern Nigeria and the Tiv in central Nigeria, neither of whom had state structures, were a mystery to them, and they tried to impose regular chiefs on them who could act as negotiators and servants of the colonial administration.

There is little question that in nonstate societies at the stage where growing population densities increase the level of social conflict and crowding there is considerable ferment and discontent. People sense that they are becoming more dependent on leaders who use their power to grab more resources and exert greater power. Humans do not naturally like to follow orders, hand over much of what they produce, and lose their independence, though in the thousands of years of agrarian societies most people had to learn to be humble and accept the power of their leaders.

Among the Tiv in central Nigeria, for example, anthropologists found a society on the verge of creating a state. Until then, this had been avoided because the Tiv could expand as they overcrowded, but by the time they were absorbed into colonial Nigeria, that situation was coming to a close. Some individuals were accumulating greater wealth and power as leaders, and the Tiv were convinced that such individuals possessed a magical, evil organ inside their bodies that gave them access to power. The Tiv were on the verge of what might well have been an involuntary, resented, but nevertheless necessary change to a state society.

The same was true among the Ibo in southeastern Nigeria. By the late nineteenth century there was a high population density, and the Ibo were in contact with neighbors who had developed states much earlier. There existed secret societies in which leading men were enrolled to act as influential leaders. In particular, there was an oracle in the heart of Ibo country to which people appealed to settle disputes. This oracle was run by a particularly powerful secret society that demanded payments for its advice and mediation and had a kind of secret police to enforce its demands and decisions. The Ibo were actually on the verge of creating powerful state institutions, and we know that ordinary people greatly feared the oracle's power even as they were becoming ever more dependent on it and subject to its domination.

We have further proof that passing the threshold from prestate to state societies was a difficult, conflict-ridden process. In the recently formed state societies studied by anthropologists and historians, we almost invariably find extreme levels of cruelty carried out by the leaders against their people and even against their own kin in order to awe the general population into submission. Human sacrifice is not at all uncommon in such early state societies, and we know from archaeology that the same was true in the very earliest states in such places as Sumeria five thousands years ago and Shang China from three thousand to four thousand years ago. In early states leaders felt obliged to overawe their subjects in order to impose what must have been rather new and unpopular forms of coercion, taxation, and inequality. Later states, better established, and sanctioned by many generations of tradition, were no longer obliged to engage in human sacrifice or wanton displays of cruelty and humiliation in order to keep their subjects in line, or at least not quite so regularly.

What was happening among the Tiv and Ibo in the late nineteenth and early twentieth centuries must be roughly similar to what happened in Sumeria somewhat before 3000 B.C., in Egypt a few centuries later, and later in the Indus valley, in the Yellow River valley in northern China, in the valleys of highland Mexico, and in the narrow valleys of Peru that ran from the Andes mountains to the Pacific. These were the places where the first states came into being spontaneously. Later states were created through contact with or at least knowledge about other states.

It is not surprising that the earliest states we know about, in Sumeria, consisted of cities made up of granaries, temples, and the fortifications built around them for protection. The mediator-shaman-priests began to build temples from which to exercise their craft and power, and they needed granaries in order to store the tribute they took from people to pay them for their efforts. Their allies, the soldiers, who were becoming professional war makers, also benefited from this tribute. They manned the walls that protected the temple-storehouses, they enforced the decisions of the priests, and they fought neighboring states competing for the same resources. The first rulers were priest-warrior-kings. But once in place, they did not simply continue to levy tribute for their services. Armed with greater wealth, with a professional soldiery, and with the sanctioning power of the priests, they took a lot more, warring with their neighbors to expand their taxable base and subjecting the peasants under

their control to ever harsher tribute and discipline. After a few generations, the kings no longer were just interpreters of divine will, but claimed
divinity themselves and became god-kings.

By the time the more successful of these kings had managed to
conquer their less successful rivals and create larger territories, they
could command the resources necessary to build truly splendid royal
cities, palaces, and tombs. This was the stage at which the Sumerians
united their little city states into real kingdoms and eventually an empire.
At a similar stage of state development, the Egyptian pharaohs and
Central American states built their pyramids and great cities. Under such
rulers, human institutions took on a shape that was unlike anything ever
seen before, but that remained the prevailing way of setting up social
systems for thousands of years to come.

Class, Status, and Force: Increasing Inequality and Making It Hereditary

Long before states there were some individuals who commanded greater
respect, awe, or fear from others. The prestige that was associated with
this could be passed on by heredity, and there were lineages—families—
that were thought to be particularly apt as shamans or leaders. But
heredity was a weak basis for influence in prestate societies because there
was little to pass on other than respect. Performance of great feats
depended on the individual's ability. But, once it became possible to
inherit property and other forms of wealth, then power could be passed
on, too. It became possible to buy allegiance and to will this capacity to
descendants. Permanent staffs of soldiers, priests, and courtiers attached
to the royal personage remained available for use by the heir of the dead
king, whether a direct offspring, a sibling, a spouse, or some other relative.

We might ask why people want to leave their wealth, their privileges,
or their positions to their relatives. There is no good answer to this other
than to say that on the whole, this is the way we are. That most of us try
to favor those to whom we are related is probably related to a deep,
biologically determined imperative to help some of our genes survive.
Other animals and all living organisms clearly respond to this imperative,
which may be the master principle behind all evolution. Those organisms
that lack it reproduce less successfully and their descendants are more
likely to die out.

Not only do we seek to pass on our advantages to our closest relatives,
but also most of us are willing to believe that children of important people

share some of their attributes. Everywhere that states developed, the notion also existed that leadership of the state was properly passed on within the lineage, or family of the ruler. There were also lineages of priests and of high officials. And though there might be competition between highly placed lineages for the position of the king, it was only rarely, through some unexpected turn of events such as outside invasion, revolutions, or other catastrophes, that entirely new royal lineages sprang up suddenly.

Societies with states became what sociologists called *stratified*, that is, divided into fairly stable ranks into which all the members of the society were placed, from very high to very low, and these rankings became largely hereditary. It was possible to shift from one rank to another, but to rise above one's birth took special effort, skill, and luck.

Human societies have three ways of stratifying themselves. The first is by sheer wealth and possessions. Those who own more resources, especially productive ones, have greater power than those who do not. This is called class, or economic power. But it was only later, in societies that specialized in trade, and much later in modern capitalist societies, that class became the main basis of stratification. Originally, it was a combination of prestige and force that made some powerful and others weak, and it was access to that prestige and force, in the form of temples over which to preside and soldiers to command, that distinguished the elites of early states from the commoners.

Prestige, or status, is much more difficult to measure than wealth or class position. Clearly, when shamans began to use their influence to collect payment for their services, used this to hire guards and enforcers, and established early states, they relied heavily on their ability to command seemingly awesome supernatural abilities. On the other hand, without a firmer basis of power, status is quickly dissipated. Some commoners are not awed and may refuse to follow orders or make payment, and unless there exists a permanent body of enforcers, status becomes at best a basis for respect, not for the enormous differentials in power that developed in early states.

Power is the ability to command, and ultimately, all state power rests on the state's capacity to command physical force to ensure obedience. Those who seize resources by using their prestige may make themselves rich, but without force to back them up they will not be able to keep their property.

On the other hand it is easier, cheaper, and safer to exercise power over subjects who think it fair and right that some should be high and most others low. Ruling groups with high prestige, that is with high status, have an easier time maintaining their power than those who must rely solely on brute force. Similarly, those with access to wealth find it easier to buy allegiance and to keep their property if they command both force and high status. In stable states that emerged, status, based on the assumption that certain individuals had a natural right to rule, usually because they were the descendants of those who had ruled before them and so had godly sanction for their superiority, went along with high class position and the command of force. But when these three sources of social power were separated, as they could be, great instability occurred.

If conquering warriors entered a society, they might strip the old power holders of both their property and their control over force, but it took longer to destroy their prestige. If groups of merchants or officials accumulated enough wealth without having the status of older elites, strains could develop. Or a rebellious group of peasants, overtaxed by their betters, might rise up in exasperation and momentarily destroy the balance of force that had kept the state intact. Incongruities between status, class, and the command of force produced much of the high political drama in agrarian societies.

There are many instances of such incongruities that led to severe political conflict. For example, Julius Caesar in the middle of the first century B.C. had the political support of ordinary Roman citizens but was opposed by the old Roman aristocracy. Yet Caesar had command of a powerful army, and he imposed his will on Rome. A desperate group of aristocrats murdered him, but to no avail. Caesar's heirs were able to mobilize both more popular support and more soldiers than the old elite, and they imposed their rule on Rome, changing it from a republic run by a tiny elite of landowners to an empire run by whoever could control the army. This was one of the most momentous political changes in the ancient world, yet it did not change the fundamental structure of society, only the makeup of the elite.

At this point it suffices to say that the great innovation of states was not only to create relatively stable government, but to stratify society into different status groups, classes, and power holders. The highest of the high, the pharaohs and emperors, obtained extraordinary privileges and could lead spectacularly luxurious lives. At the other end, the ordinary peasants, who formed well over 90 percent of the population of most agrarian societies, actually fell to positions lower than their ancestors who had been free of states. More of their produce and work was taken from them, they were forced to humble themselves and take orders, and they were gradually defined as almost a different species than members of the small elite—mere subhumans. Officials ranging from high priests, nobles, and military leaders to lower officials, merchants, and soldiers formed various strata or social levels between the royal families at the top and the lowly, barely human peasants at the bottom. Of course, with war and increasing social stratification, slavery also developed, and it was possible for slaves to be considered even lower than ordinary peasants, though in the Islamic world some slaves used as professional soldiers took power on their own and turned themselves into hereditary elites.

In agrarian societies, the scale and complexity of social organization was far greater than in prestate societies. The procreative family remained a basic unit, but most people lived in villages rather than small bands (though the royal palace and the government were usually based in larger cities). All sorts of other institutions were developed to bind societies together: temples and priesthoods, lineages of nobles, armies, associations of merchants and of other specialized professions such as clerks or prostitutes, various departments of government to handle irrigation, foreign relations, the king's wardrobe, and so on.

It is only with the development of modern capitalist societies since the late eighteenth and early nineteenth centuries that the bulk of humanity has ceased to be stratified according to these ancient patterns first developed in the early states in the fourth, third, and second millennium B.C. Even today, we have kept many of the same kinds of organizations, though modern societies are no longer so unevenly divided between a very small elite at the top and a large mass of very poor, exploited peasants below them.

Nomads, Migrants, and Other Raiders

States did not develop in isolation. Around each of the original states there were other peoples, sometimes speaking similar languages, but with lower population densities and different ways of sustaining themselves. Nomadism—that is, living by herding domesticated animals such as cattle, sheep, or goats—developed (but not in the Americas) at about the same time as agriculture, and most nomads needed to exchange products with sedentary agriculturists in order to survive. In the deserts and dry savannahs that surrounded the early states in the Middle East, or north of China, or in the deserts and mountains north and west of the Indus valley these nomadic peoples quickly picked up the metallurgy of the more advanced states. But with their greater mobility and hardiness they became formidable raiders who could endanger their more stratified, more numerous settled neighbors. A pattern developed quite early in which they would raid the cities in order to obtain the greater luxuries of the established state elites, and sometimes they could sweep away ruling groups and place themselves at the head of the states. Endless war was the price of maintaining states under such circumstances. The attraction of all the luxury and the availability of peasants who could be taxed and used as a resource, just like domesticated animals, was too great for the nomads to resist. When ruling state dynasties were strong, they would send expeditions into nomadic areas to tame and control the nomads. When they were weakened by internal divisions or by sloth, the menace around their borders would grow. Partly it was a matter of natural weather cycles too. In good times the nomads' flocks would increase. Then they and their animals would overpopulate their grazing grounds, and when the inevitable few years of drought would follow they would have to invade neighboring kingdoms to escape ruin.

This is how Semitic-speaking wanderers from Palestine invaded Egypt and set up a new ruling dynasty in the seventeenth century B.C. These people, the Hyksos, may have been urban dwellers, but they used related tribesmen who were nomads as allies. At that time the Hebrews were one such tribe of nomads dependent on their flocks more than on agriculture. In a time of drought, they migrated into Egypt as allies of the Hyksos, and their settlement there is reflected in the biblical story of Joseph. They were a favored people at this time in Egypt but were later relegated to subservient status when a native Egyptian dynasty regained control in the sixteenth century B.C.

About three thousand years later, Ibn Khaldoun, a North African historian, set out a whole theory of historical cycles based on the periodic conquest of the settled, luxurious cities on the North African coast by mountain and desert nomads who would conquer, rule, and gradually degenerate from soft living. A similar cycle seemed to occur in China as well, with nomadic Turks and Mongols playing the same role as Semitic nomads in the Middle East or Arab and Berber raiders in North Africa. And the history of Persia shows a similar pattern, starting with the Aryan (Iranian) invasions as long ago as about 2200 B.C. (Aryans spoke languages related to those of the groups who peopled most of Europe and later India, so that their large language family is known as Indo-European.) Later, other Aryan, Arabic, Turkic, and Mongol peoples invaded Persia, but Persia's Indo-European language remains its dominant tongue to this day.

The Indus valley was also subjected to periodic invasions by cattle herders from central Asia, starting with Aryan invaders in about 1600

B.C., whose mythologized chronicles, the Rig-Veda, became the defining texts of later Indian culture. Later other central Asian peoples—the Sakas, the Kushan, White Huns, Turks, Mongols, and various Afghan tribes— periodically invaded northern India and set up new kingdoms and ruling dynasties. The last of these were the Mughals, a Persianized group of mixed Turks and Mongols who took over and ruled most of India from the sixteenth to the eighteenth century A.D.

At the start of the nineteenth century A.D., urban Fulani in what is now northern Nigeria used their alliance with their nomadic kinfolk to conquer the old Hausa city states of the region and set up a new empire. Thus we see that this ancient pattern of conquest, remarkably similar to that shown in the story of Joseph in Egypt, persisted to the dawn of the industrial, modern age in many parts of the world.

State structures with permanent leadership, hereditary kings, and a large military force could be wielded as a raiding force much more easily than prestate, less formal structures. The neighbors of the great states saw this, so the institution of the state spread around the borders of the early states even where the original conditions that produced states did not apply. For example, from Sumeria state institutions spread throughout the Middle East. Egypt, which may have developed independently or been influenced by Sumeria, in turn influenced the lands to its south, in what is now the Sudan, and from there, with time, state institutions spread south into parts of eastern Africa and west across the Sahelian region south of the Sahara. From China the idea of the state moved to the northeast into Korea and Japan, to the north and west into Mongolia and central Asia, and south into Vietnam. From northern India state institutions spread to the rest of India and in the first millennium A.D. to Southeast Asia as far as Java and Bali. Similar expansion of state institutions radiated from their starting points in Mexico and Peru to Central America and along the Andes Mountains. Almost certainly, however, the reason for the relatively slow spread of state institutions was that most people resisted, as much as they could, the imposition of forced stratification, so that simply observing the existence of states did not convert nonstate people immediately. But if they wanted to raid states or protect themselves against expansive ones, they eventually had no choice but to organize themselves in this way too and give greater power to a set of permanent leaders who could coordinate their war making and hold together shifting tribal alliances.

Neighboring nomads and raiders were not the only threats to early states. The advantages of being rulers, high nobles, and officials in states were so great compared to those of being mere commoners that people struggled fiercely for that right. From the very beginning of state histories we know that family members plotted against and killed each other to obtain high office, and that families fought bitterly against each other to gain or retain high status or wealth.

The powerful were in effect milking the ordinary people, and when elites overpopulated by reproducing too successfully, the human resources on which they depended were strained and had to be fought over, just like hunting or agricultural lands earlier. Thus the political life of agrarian states was filled with plots and fratricidal civil wars, with invasions from migrating, different peoples, and with wars between neighboring states as elites tried to expand their resource base in order to ensure their survival. In fact, most conventional history consists of stories about these events, though the historical chronicles of these societies rarely explain the pressures that drove state elites to behave in such warlike ways. Stories are told as individual morality tales, and we are left to figure out what really drove these societies to such violence.

The state, born of increasing social conflict and war, continued for most of its existence as a machine for brutally exploiting most of its people, making war with its neighbors, and provoking internal, violent competition among its elites. There was, however, much more to agrarian states. They also built the first great human civilizations, with elaborate high cultures, complex artistic forms of expression, sophisticated theologies and sciences, and spectacular rituals that continue to amaze us in what seems to be a more prosaic and democratic postagrarian age.

Great Cultures:
The Moral Basis of Agrarian Civilizations

Each of the original centers of state formation developed lasting high cultures. Those in the Americas were largely though not entirely obliterated by the European invasions in the middle of the second millennium; but those in the Old World persist to this day, though of course they have continued to change and adapt since they came into being thousands of years ago. The writing of the ancient Sumerians, after many modifications, eventually became the alphabets of the eastern Mediterranean, which evolved into the Greek and Latin alphabets used by Europeans. Another branch developed into the Arabic alphabet, which is used not only by Arabic and Persian speakers today but in religious texts wherever there is an Islamic community. The ideograms used by the early Chinese civilizations evolved into the characters that spread across all of East Asia and continue to be used in modern China and Japan. India developed an alphabet, probably derived originally from the Middle East by way of Persia, that spread in modified form to all the Indian languages and then throughout Southeast Asia, where forms of it are still used by the Burmese, Thais, and Khmer.

The spread of writing systems was only one aspect of the cultures of the early states. There were also whole conceptions of how life should be lived, of religion, of statecraft, of musical and artistic expression, and, of course, of technology. In watching Javanese shadow puppet plays today one is seeing very ancient stories that are two to three thousand years old about politics and love in distant Indian courts of that time. In reading the biblical story of Noah and the great flood we are looking at a tale first told at least five thousand years ago in Sumeria where there were real floods in the Tigris and Euphrates Valleys of what is now Iraq. And when Lee Kuan Yew, the former president of Singapore, told his people in the 1980s and 1990s that they should study Confucianism as a guide to a better life in the late twentieth century, he was referring to many centuries of commentaries about texts supposedly originally written twenty-five hundred years ago in China.

This is not to say that the cultural forms elaborated thousands of years ago have remained unchanged, or that what we believe to be their message is exactly what they wrote or felt at that time. On the contrary, culture evolves and changes all the time. But the starting point for most modern cultures lies somewhere in these ancient centers whose influence spread far beyond their original boundaries.

For most of the time that humans existed, they lived primarily by gathering and hunting, so that we are physically still built for such lives even though practically no humans live that way now. We have evolved physically rather little since then. Similarly, we have evolved culturally from agrarian societies that were highly stratified, dangerously crowded, ridden by violent conflicts, and engaged in almost permanent war. Over the past five thousand years most humans have lived in such societies, and it is from them that modern civilizations evolved. Thus many of our deepest beliefs and cultural attributes still come from these venerable civilizations, even though most of the world no longer really lives according to such arrangements. Human culture evolves much more quickly than human biology, but some parts of our culture in the past few centuries have changed much more slowly than some other parts, so that we continue to be influenced by a past most of us know very poorly even though it permeates our daily lives.

What has come down to us was primarily the culture of the elite, what was elaborated by the priests, warriors, nobles, officials, and kings of the ancient world. Yet at the same time that they worked out a high culture of their own, these people had to keep their populations under control, and they were always looking for ways of legitimating their rule and the blatant inequality and unfairness of agrarian society. It was not an easy matter to create belief systems that brought the needs of elites and commoners together. Often, this was done by blending older village practices and ideas with high culture, so that today we continue to mix these ancient traditions. Christmas, for example, long antedates Christianity in that it celebrates the passing of the winter solstice. It combines old European and more recent Christian practices that have been modernized and adapted to our more commercial, modern culture. Throughout the Far East ancient shamanistic magic and practices underlie the sophisticated Confucian and Buddhist traditions that developed later.

Aside from being a blend of different traditions, every great cultural heritage also combines different ethical and religious attitudes developed by various classes and status groups in the classical agrarian societies. Warriors, who lived by courage and athletic skill, developed an ethical system in which bravery and honor, bold action and the grand gesture were the ideal. Clerks, the early bureaucrats and record keepers, tax collectors, and administrators of agrarian states, had a different ethic that emphasized duty to the state, a sense of responsibility for proper administration, and cultivation of the skills of reading, writing, and classification necessary for their careers.

Peasants, whether formally free, or as often happened, bound to the soil by their masters by slavery or serfdom, did not have the option of cultivating grand visions and ethical systems. Almost always illiterate, and with little or no spare time, their horizons limited by their work and restricted mobility, they developed attitudes of resignation and acceptance combined with superstitious awe of the forces that could make or break them without warning or explanation. There could be sudden wars in which they were victimized, but they were never told why these occurred or what they meant. There might be sudden droughts or floods imposed on them by a capricious nature. A nasty landowner or king might suddenly raise their taxes or kidnap their children to enslave them. None of these human or natural forces were predictable or controllable. Thus it was in peasant villages that the most ancient magical rites and superstitions persisted for millennia underneath a formal adherence to the intellectualized version of religion practiced by priestly elites.

A common practice in the early states was to try to solve the problem of divergent ethical and spiritual needs of the many social strata by recreating the human hierarchy as a divine one. The king became god, and his nobles, priests, and administrators became the intermediaries who communicated to the people; the peasants were supposed to be impressed and obey. The pyramids and giant temples built to celebrate these religions were meant to remind all the people how grand their god-kings really were.

We can tell from ancient remnants of these religious beliefs—for example, in Hinduism, Greek mythology, and what we know about Egyptian mythology—that the religious-ethical systems that were elaborated in these circumstances were filled with contradictions and inconsistencies. First, the gods they portrayed were a mixture of older, regional deities taken from the various parts of the states that had conquered and united their neighbors. Second, even though some of them were imagined as part animal and part human, their behavior tended to be much like that of the elite who were considered proper models for admiration. Peasants make few appearances in these mythologies. So there was the problem of how to provide a system of belief that might fit kings and noble warrior elites as well as clerks, merchants, peasants, and perhaps even slaves. And finally, inasmuch as the king, pharaoh, or emperor was supposed to be a deity too, the loss of a battle, the death of a king, or even the fall of a dynasty had to be explained without complete loss of faith. It was necessary to appeal to a higher deity, to a superior ethic, that placed the king at a more mortal, if still elevated, level. This was particularly critical if boundaries of states changed, as they often did. In the competition between various kings and emperors, who was to know which one was divine?

It took anywhere from one to three thousand years for the agrarian civilizations to work out solutions to these grave ethical and religious problems. All of the world's major religions come from the three areas of the Old World that were also homes to the original states: the Middle East, India, and China. In all of them, stable solutions to the problem of creating stable belief systems were worked out in the period from about 500 B.C. to 700 A.D., long after the appearance of the first states.

The astonishing thing is that the religious traditions that emerged from these three areas are so different. From the Middle East there eventually came a fierce form of monotheism in which the universe has a beginning and an end, the forces of good and evil contend with each other, and finally the forces of good win. Judaism, Zoroastrianism, Christianity, and

Islam all came from the Middle East. Middle Eastern religions promise the poor and afflicted that if they are good they will be rewarded after death, and explain that all the suffering and cruelty on earth are part of a greater plan through which God tests each individual.

Middle Eastern religions have a greater capacity than other religious traditions for producing millenarian, utopian ideologies—that is, visions of a future in which final redemption is possible through the arrival of a truth-telling prophet. It is not surprising, then, that even in the modern world the two most apocalyptic, millenarian, and fanatical new political ideologies of the twentieth century, namely Marxism and fascism, came out of the Judeo-Christian world. And in the late twentieth century, the most militant ideology on earth, now that Marxism has collapsed, is fundamentalist Islam.

Indian religion stressed instead the unending, repetitive nature of the universe. All creatures are reborn, and those who are good get reborn as progressively higher and higher forms of life, eventually becoming elevated humans who, if they accumulate enough merit, can escape endless rebirth and the pain of living by moving into a higher state of being in which they are entirely removed from the eternal cycle of life, death, and rebirth.

Though Buddhism was born in India, it did not last there. Instead, the older Hindu tradition of religion, without a united theology or a coherent prophetic message, reasserted itself. Buddhism did spread to the east and south, where it was mixed with other aspects of the Indian religious tradition, particularly in Southeast Asia. But Indian religion did not move toward any kind of monotheism, or toward a conception of a universe with a logical beginning and end, a universe in which all history has a God-given purpose.

In China something else happened. The empire's administrators invented their own religion, which stressed social ethics and responsibility rather than a divine plan or godly intervention. Confucianism never became a mass religion, and in fact, despite its acknowledgment of divine forces, it is hardly a religion at all if compared to the theologically driven Middle Eastern and European religions that make such sweeping, universal claims for their gods and their own versions of history. But at the same time other religious forms developed in China and the part of the world it influenced. A modified form of Buddhism was imported from India, and Taoism, a combination of ethical principles, magic, and science, competed with and sometimes blended with Confucianism and ancient ancestor worship to produce a mixture that resembles neither the systematized, dogmatic, unilinear monotheism of the Middle East and Europe nor the fatalistic Indian sense that everything has happened before and will happen again in an unending cycle.

We will see later that the differences in these three great religious traditions and further divisions within them may have had a significant impact on social change in the modern era. Because they have proved to be so long lasting, they will continue to influence future change as well.

This brief account cannot begin to do justice to the many strands that developed in each of these areas, with special versions of religions for different classes and strata of society, with regional peculiarities and changes over many generations, and with centuries of learned commentary and elaboration. But underneath all this, it needs to be said that the Indian and Chinese traditions tended, on the whole, to be more tolerant of splits and local variations because these could be accommodated into their world view more easily. The Middle Eastern tradition, which became the Christian tradition in Europe and eventually the Islamic one in the Middle East, was and has continued to be more insistent on a single uniform orthodoxy. This does not mean that there were no splits or variations; it implies that such divisions were particularly troublesome and the cause of many conflicts and further changes.

The Problem of Administration and the Cycle of Political Decay and Reconstruction

Transforming religious thought into a more coherent, more generalizable form that could hold together the elites of agrarian states and offer solace to the oppressed majorities was not the only difficult problem that had to be solved in order to stabilize agrarian states and make them work more efficiently. There was also the problem of the inevitable tensions between kings and their administrators, nobles, and priests as well as between the capital of the state and the outlying provinces. The larger the agrarian state, the greater the problem. It was not until many centuries of statecraft that it became possible to create the very large empires that eventually took over most of the ancient world's human population.

Part of the problem was transportation. Advances came with improvement in the use of oars and sails in ships. On land the invention of the wheeled cart and the domestication and improved use of horses, cattle, and later camels made long-distance travel and transportation possible. In the Americas, with no available substitute for horses or cattle except for the small and far less useful llamas in the Andes, transportation did not make these advances, though the use of runners on a developed road system made possible a gigantic Inca Empire in the fifteenth century A.D.

But the technology of administration also had to be developed, and this is a social, not a mechanical skill. One of the chief problems, which was never entirely solved by agrarian states, even as late as China in the early twentieth century, was that of a natural tension between the center and periphery. Local notables in the provinces had every incentive to keep as much of the revenue as possible that they collected from local peasants or taxes on trade. After all, they faced the problems of providing for their own luxuries and supporting their own retainers, soldiers, priests, and relatives as a force to keep order. The king in the capital city, however, needed all the revenue he could obtain, and he or his staff had to find a way of ensuring that the provinces did not withhold too much. Otherwise the center got weak, and a provincial lord who succeeded in building up his own force would threaten to overthrow the dynasty and become the ruler. Even if provincial governors did not take over the center, they might secede, and secession could so weaken the empire that it became subject to raids and eventually collapsed. This happened countless times in all the great agrarian empires.

It was this kind of internal division that allowed Germanic tribes to destroy the Roman Empire in western Europe in the fifth century A.D., or the Hyksos to take over Egypt in the seventeenth century B.C. It was when China was divided or in the midst of civil war that it was most vulnerable to conquest by northern nomads. A somewhat different but relevant example is that the Spaniards were able to conquer the Inca Empire with astounding ease because it had just split and was in the midst of a civil war in the early sixteenth century. Had it been united at the time, the history of South America might have taken a quite different turn.

To ensure political stability, techniques had to be worked out to control tensions between provincial notables and the center, as well as between the king's need for revenues and those demanded by his tax-collecting officials or representatives. The Chinese only partially solved this problem in the third century B.C., and even then the same tensions kept on reappearing until the end of imperial rule in 1911.

In the Middle East, there was a tendency for ever larger imperial structures to form as the techniques of statecraft improved. After the Egyptian kingdom, which was generally limited to the Nile valley, the first large empire was that of the Akkadians in the twenty-third century

B.C. But it was not until the Hittites from the seventeenth to the thirteenth century B.C. and even more the Assyrians from the thirteenth to the seventh century B.C. that large-scale empires became a regular feature of the political landscape. Those who finally perfected the technique of ruling very large empires, after the fall of the Assyrians, were the Persians in the sixth century B.C. Their administrative system was taken over and improved by Greek conquerors led by Alexander of Macedonia, whose successors ruled the eastern Mediterranean from the fourth century B.C. until they were conquered by the Romans and Parthians two to three hundred years later.

It may not be just a coincidence that highly stable solutions to the problems of running large agrarian empires were most satisfactorily solved at about the same time by the Chinese and the Mediterranean civilizations. In China in the third century B.C., at about the same time that the Romans were becoming the greatest power in the Western world, the first unified Chinese empire was established by Qin Shi Huangdi. Beginning in 221 B.C., he ruled the kingdom of Qin, which had existed for almost five hundred years and had been slowly consolidating and improving its system of administration. The immediate successors of his dynasty, the Han, who took power in 202 B.C., ruled China until the third century A.D. within boundaries that were roughly similar to those of modern China. Rome, which had been a slowly growing power in Italy for almost three hundred years, became master of the western Mediterranean in 202 B.C. and of the eastern Mediterranean over the next one hundred fifty years.

In both cases, centralized bureaucracies had to be created in order to rule these empires. In China, the local nobles who had made centralized rule impossible had to be destroyed before a bureaucratic, centralized empire could be established. In Rome, a republican form of government dominated by a small but contentious elite was eliminated and replaced first by military dictators and then by emperors in the late first century B.C. And at about the same time, in the fourth and third century B.C., the first large united Indian empire was created by the Mauryas, though in the case of India this proved to be an impermanent arrangement.

In other words, the major classical empires encompassing vast numbers of individuals and able to bring some sort of unity to different linguistic and ethnic groups became practical only after about 1000 B.C., and it was not until the fourth and third centuries B.C. that the greatest powers of the ancient world, Rome and China, coalesced. For all this to happen there had to be sufficiently high population densities, which meant improvements in agricultural technology. There had to be bureaucrats who knew how to keep good records. There had to be adequate transportation and solid weapons. The spread of iron working in the Middle East beginning in about 1000 B.C., and from there to China about five hundred years later, played a role in the progress of military technology. Such grand empires and civilizations would not have been possible in the earlier stages of agrarian states.

It is suggestive that in the Americas, too, it took a very long time for empires to learn how to rule large territories. It was only a couple of centuries before the arrival of the Spaniards that the Inca Empire, which ruled on a scale as vast as that of the major agrarian empires in the Old World, united most of Andean South America. Its natural history was cut short by the arrival of the Europeans, who destroyed it in the sixteenth century, so we cannot know what it would have turned into. But the absence of available beasts of burden hindered progress in transportation and agriculture that might have doomed the American civilizations to lag far behind those of the Old World even if Europeans had not intruded when they did.

Several different types of institutions were tried to hold together large agrarian states. It was possible to use officials who were rotated regularly so that they could never gain enough local support to threaten the power of the center. But paying them was problematic in economies that generated little spare cash. Usually such officials were allowed to take a portion of the taxes they collected. It became common in Rome, for example, to purchase governorships and the rights to collect taxes, and anything above what the central government expected to get was profit. Such a system gave provincial governors every incentive to take too much from their district, because after their term was over they would leave. Allowing officials to exploit a particular territory as if it were theirs but then forcing them to give it up is called a *prebendal* system of administration.

Another possibility was to let officials stay in one region a long time, and even gain proprietary rights to a region. Though the center always fought this, at times it could not be avoided because the local governors simply became too powerful to remove. If they then obtained the right to keep and pass on the territory to their descendants, they became hereditary owners of their provinces. This system is called *feudalism.*

Between the prebendal system, which overexploited the territory under an administrator's control, and the feudal system, in which administrators turned into hereditary lords, there were all sorts of compromises, but these were the two extremes between which agrarian states alternated. The long history of Egypt, for example, finds periods in which the center was strong, followed by the gradual strengthening of local lords and feudalization, followed by new periods of central strength. The Roman Empire, after solving this problem for several centuries, gradually disintegrated as the aristocracy turned itself from urban dwellers competing for office to rural ones living on their estates and withholding taxes from the weakening center. By the fifth century A.D., what had been a prebendal system of administration had turned into something close to a feudal one, especially in its western portion, and centralized rule ended.

China went through a number of such cycles too, and eventually more or less solved the problem by creating a professional bureaucracy that obtained office and promotion by passing exams. This literate elite studied the Confucian texts and commentaries in order to pass the exams, and when individuals entered the imperial bureaucracy, they were supposed to be assigned to provinces other than the ones where they were born. It was the success of this bureaucratic system that always brought China back together after periods of disunity, because the various local kings or nomads who conquered pieces of China used these officials as their administrators. It was the bureaucrats who carried the notion of a united Chinese empire and civilization and taught their political masters that it was always desirable to put China back together.

No other territorial unit of comparable size managed to hold together, or rather, reassemble itself after splitting as long as China, and this is why today China encompasses such a huge area containing so many people with a common culture. Egypt accomplished a comparable feat, holding itself together, or always reuniting, no matter who ruled it, for at least three thousand years until it was conquered by Rome. But Egypt encompasses only one river valley. At its height it only contained one tenth as many people as China during the Han dynasty in the first century A.D.

Much later, the Ottoman Empire, which was the greatest power in the eastern Mediterranean region from the fifteenth to the early nineteenth centuries A.D., tried to solve the problem of training a loyal bureaucracy by using slave boys taken from its Christian subjects, converting them to Islam, and sending them through rigorous schooling. The idea was that slaves cut off from their3 families would have to be loyal to the central government and, if they performed well, could aspire to great rewards. But this institution was eventually corrupted as Muslim Turkish families conspired to get their sons into these schools. The empire ceased to produce loyal servants and became subject to the common ill of bureaucratic corruption in which officials took increasing amounts of revenue from the center. This led to decreasing efficiency, a less capable army, the decline of the empire, and a kind of feudalization in which provincial governors tried to subvert the power of the central government.

These kinds of administrative problems did not involve only the elites. On the contrary, they could have severe consequences for the masses of ordinary peasants. Administrations under stress—that is, receiving insufficient funds—would increase taxes, and this could easily ruin the peasants who lived close to the edge of subsistence in the best of times. Pushed beyond a certain limit, peasants, who normally kept out of politics, had no choice but to rebel or starve. China was subject to periodic massive peasant uprisings that threatened and sometimes destroyed the empire, or at least its ruling dynasty.

The problem was that decreasing revenues for the center encouraged greater use of force to extract higher taxes, and the ensuing misery and rebellion required even greater military expenditures, until eventually poorly paid armies turned into bandits themselves and further threatened both the peasantry and the power of the center. Whether in China or Rome, or later in medieval England and France, or in Imperial Russia and the Ottoman Empire in the seventeenth and eighteenth centuries, contemporary accounts describe bloody uprisings, wandering bandits and mercenaries, and the cyclical return of great "times of trouble." We will soon see that when the fragile structure of agrarian monarchies disintegrated, this could often be accompanied by a whole series of other miseries: wars, plagues, great depopulations, and sometimes the virtual collapse of entire societies.

Though the classical agrarian empires partially solved the problem of administering states, it was not until industrial societies developed in the nineteenth century that the level of economic activity became high enough to support permanent, paid bureaucracies without having to periodically ruin the population and threaten disintegration. Only with industrial societies did it finally become possible to pay all officials in cash instead of letting them loose on poor peasants. Also, the increase in productivity was such that in industrialized countries since the nineteenth century the vast majority of people have risen well above mere subsistence. However onerous they may find their taxes, few people in industrial societies risk starving because of them.

It was in response to administrative exigencies that the Chinese developed their Confucian bureaucratic system with its own distinctive ethic and culture, that the Persians invented a system of secret police spies to report on the activities of provincial satraps or governors, and that the late Roman Empire recognized the enormous attraction of Christianity as both a solace for the poor and as a way of disciplining the elite, and so made it the official state religion. This last act, it should be noted, did not save the western portion of the empire from dissolution, but it preserved the Eastern (Greek-speaking) Roman Empire, which continued to be a major power for seven centuries after the fall of western Europe to Germanic invaders.

It is possible to think of administrative innovations or the adoption of new beliefs and social practices as evolutionary mutations. Some worked, and others did not. Over time, those traits that worked were kept. Sometimes these were due to conquest by outsiders, sometimes to deliberate, planned changes by the elites, and at other times to spontaneous adaptation by the population itself.

Each state adopted its own institutions. But all faced somewhat parallel problems, and it turned out that only a narrow range of solutions was possible.

Republics were tried—making a body chosen from members of the status and class elites of the society responsible for power instead of a single ruler or ruling family. This worked very well in some smaller states, particularly Mediterranean trading cities. It failed as an administrative solution for bigger units, and the greatest republic in the ancient world, Rome, became a monarchy ruled by an emperor at the time of Christ. (Rome actually began as a monarchy when it was small but overthrew its kings and became a republic ruled by elite families until Julius Caesar's successors subdued the Roman Senate and curtailed its powers.) Surely it is not a coincidence that eventually every successful agrarian state evolved into a hereditary monarchy.

During the Song dynasty in the tenth to eleventh centuries, China reached a very high level of technological, scientific, and general cultural sophistication. Some historians believe it might have been on the verge of a modernizing period of growth that would have made China the world's first industrial, scientific society. But the bureaucratic elite tended to devalue the military too much. It was not so much that there was no army, because there was a large one, but that professional soldiers were accorded little prestige, and leading officers were frequently rotated so that they would be unable to get to know their men and build up individual power bases. This proved to be the undoing of the dynasty. The army was too inefficient to hold back invasions by the Ruzhen from Manchuria, who conquered the Song's northern provinces and brought to a stop China's promising development for several centuries. This is an example of cultural attitudes and administrative practices that became dysfunctional.

Many other examples can be given. In the eleventh century the Eastern Roman or Byzantine Empire was the strongest power in the entire Mediterranean. But the emperors were unable to prevent local landowners from seizing great estates. In the process, along the border regions, the independent peasantry, which had provided the soldiers to maintain the borders, was destroyed. It lost its lands to the nobility, and consequently its willingness to fight for the empire. This left the borders open, and in the late eleventh century an invasion by Seljuk Turks swept into Anatolia. Though the Byzantine Empire partially recovered, it never regained its strength, and it gradually faded away.

Of course in the long run all agrarian systems failed because from one of them, in western Europe, a new type of society developed that made agrarian states and social systems obsolete. But the interesting question is, first, why did some agrarian systems and states adapt so much better than others? Second, how did some succeed in being so innovative, evolving into new types of societies, while most others, even among the relatively successful, stagnated and ultimately failed? We will address these question later in this chapter, and in more detail in Chapter 3.

The Conservatism of Village Life

For the vast majority of people in agrarian societies, life went on with seemingly few changes except for periodic disruptions from the outside. Peasant villages worked out solutions to the problems of raising food, surviving in a hostile world, reproducing, and taking what enjoyment they could from their culture. Very often these were remarkably stable solutions that worked for centuries or even millennia without too much change.

Both European tradition and traditions from other high centers of civilization hold that peasants are unresponsive, bound by tradition, and incapable of changing. This stereotypical view became especially prevalent among Europeans in the nineteenth and twentieth centuries as they observed the rapidity of change in their own industrial economies and compared it to resistance to change put up by some of their peasants and especially by peasants in the agrarian societies conquered by the Europeans. Karl Marx raged against rural imbecility and commended the English for breaking apart village communities in India so that progress could occur.

As with many stereotypes, there was much truth to this perception of peasant life but also considerable misunderstanding of the situation. It was neither stupidity nor a mere matter of being bound to tradition that made peasants resistant to change. In each village people had become used to local variations in climate and soils, and knew, on average, how to grow what they needed. Trying new seeds or crops was a risky business. Changing to different ways of organizing production, to untested techniques, could bring swift disaster.

We know that agricultural technologies did change over time, and highly useful crops such as potatoes or maize introduced from the New World to the Old in the sixteenth and seventeenth centuries spread throughout much of Europe and Asia in the following two centuries. Some of these changes were made by elite landowners, but many were spontaneous and unplanned except by the many peasants who just made them.

Yet change was slow, and generally resisted for the simple reason that life for villagers was so dangerous. Everyone knew that sudden droughts or floods, storms, insect pests, or the even more dangerous human pests that abounded—warriors, tax collectors, feuding kings, and grasping landlords—could bring swift ruin. James Scott's research among peasants in Southeast Asia in the twentieth century has demonstrated that this produced an ethic of survival. Communities stuck together, held to tried and tested ways, were suspicious of outsiders, and sought to minimize and spread risk as opposed to trying to maximize production by taking chances.

Most people, even in industrial societies, live this way within the confines of their own social system, but in industrial societies, few people live so close to the margin that they cannot afford to try something new, and entrepreneurial risk taking can bring very substantial rewards to a far larger proportion of the population than was the case in agrarian societies. Particularly in peasant villages, the scope for innovation and behaving in a way that stands out is very small.

Along with conservatism in their economic lives, of course, peasants were also conservative in their social lives. Ancient family patterns persisted for long periods of time. Marriageable children were traded with other families and villages in order to gain alliances and spread risks in case one family was struck by disaster. Personal emotions—loves and hatreds, jealousies and sudden passions—had to be kept under control lest they split village communities or families in catastrophic ways. Unlike the Amazonian Yanomamö, who could split villages and emigrate to new stretches of uncultivated forest when conflict broke out, most developed agrarian societies had a shortage of new land, and migration was often prohibited by the authorities, who wanted to keep their tax base intact. So villages developed religious traditions and patterns of family life that downplayed passion, love, and freedom and emphasized restraint and practicality. To release tensions, every village society in the world had festival periods when people could get drunk with some drug or other, dance, and let go of their inhibitions without punishment; then all was forgotten as life returned to normal.

Such caution, which is entirely reasonable, tends to act as a brake against change. It slows the evolutionary drift of cultures. And yet, obviously, no matter how careful and conservative villagers were, or how much the higher authorities tried to keep the social and political systems stable, catastrophes did occur that were quite uncontrollable.

When natural disasters, particularly great plagues, hit the population, and when these were combined, as they usually were, with political breakdowns, major changes could occur quite rapidly. As with biological evolution, cultural evolution does not occur smoothly, but in periods of rapid, discontinuous change followed by long periods of relative stability.

The Demographic Cycle in Agrarian Societies

The origin and dissemination of great disease plagues is a subject that historians have only begun to understand in the past few decades. We now know that they actually conformed to a rough cycle. The single greatest social transformation brought about by plagues, that which occurred in the New World when Europeans brought in new diseases that may have wiped out 90 percent of the American population, was not part of any cyclical pattern, but in the Old World, and especially in Asia and Europe, somewhat of a pattern can be detected.

In an agrarian society that has solved the basic problems of administration and economic survival, the human population tends to grow. What this means is that with time increasingly marginal lands are cultivated. Irrigation works may be stretched to the limit, or people will start trying to grow their crops in drier or inferior soils, or they will move up mountain slopes. Sooner or later this invariably results in diminishing returns. Marginal soils yield less per year of labor; irrigation in dry climates produces salination of the soil; pushing cultivation up mountain slopes requires increasing amounts of work to sustain yields; hills are deforested and erosion produces more flooding downstream; fuel becomes more expensive because of deforestation; obtaining wood or charcoal for metallurgical industries—chiefly the making of weapons and tools—becomes more difficult. We see such phenomena occurring on a massive scale in the remaining crowded agrarian regions of the world today. But they happened earlier too. Italy was deforested and agricultural yields fell during the late Roman Empire; the forests grew back in the early Middle Ages because of the drastic drop in population density and then were destroyed once again with the rise of population in the late Middle Ages. Northern China suffered from erosion and diminishing returns centuries ago, and the surplus Chinese population had to emigrate to new lands in the south and in Sichuan.

Reduced crop yields might not make themselves felt at first, at least until a few bad years in the weather cycle came along. Then what had been normal droughts or floods could become catastrophic. But also, over time, with more lands being used at falling rates of return, the average amount of food available for consumption fell and the level of nutrition in the peasant population dropped.

The increase in the peasant population was likely to be accompanied by an equal or faster rise in the elite population, which had access to more food and heat. This meant that at the very moment when more and more people were eating less, the political authorities were trying to squeeze more out of them to take care of the luxurious needs of a growing number of elite individuals. Competition for resources for the elite would exacerbate internal political conflict, while eventually chronically malnourished populations would fall prey to diseases that might have left a better fed population untouched. That is how the great plagues that swept through the civilized world happened, and why they so often coincided with great wars and civil wars. Furthermore, political troubles sent armies marching through the land, and they would quickly carry diseases everywhere they went.

In the second century A.D., a great plague swept through Rome. It was probably measles. Perhaps something similar hit China at about that time. In Rome, the empire was badly weakened, though it recovered. In China, the Han dynasty was fatally weakened and soon collapsed in chaos as China split apart in the third century. It took almost three hundred years to reunite it.

In the absence of good demographic data, it is very hard, almost impossible, to know how many died in the periodic plagues that swept the civilizations of the Old World. We know that such things happened more or less regularly. Europe, central Asia, and East Asia were hit by the bubonic plague in the fourteenth century, when it is estimated that a third of Europe died. At the same time, a great European war, the Hundred Years' War between England and France, spread its own human devastation. In China in the fourteenth century the Mongol Yuan dynasty collapsed in a destructive civil war. This may have been set off and was certainly worsened by the fact that the same plague swept through central Asia (where it actually originated) and into China.

In India, because of the combination of relative crowding and the tropical climate that allows parasites to survive more easily than where cold winters kill some of them, plagues were endemic. Some analysts say that the caste system, and especially the institution of a caste of untouchables, thrived and was extended as a means for elites to try to isolate themselves from such diseases, which hit the poor and malnourished particularly hard.

We know that the combination of plagues, natural catastrophes (which were not so "natural" because they were greatly aggravated by overcropping and deforestation), and political chaos seemed to recur on a very regular basis, every two to three centuries in China. With overpopulation there was growing hunger, and the peasants in the most overcrowded areas would flee to escape crushing taxes and starvation. Revenues would drop, irrigation works would no longer be maintained, marauding, unpaid soldiers would become semibandits themselves and spread diseases as they roamed the countryside, and the ruling dynasty would be said to have lost the "Mandate of Heaven." In effect, the administrative cycle of strength and decay would occur along with and be related to the demographic cycle.

The last time this particular Chinese cycle went into operation was in the nineteenth century, when all the classic symptoms appeared: overpopulation, increasing corruption, peasant rebellions, the massive breakdown of irrigation works, and finally, in 1911, dynastic collapse followed by the country falling into anarchy and warlordism. This time, of course, the dynasty that put everything back together happened to be the Chinese Communist Party.

In Europe, the last episode like this occurred in the seventeenth century, when a series of plagues, terrible wars, especially the Thirty Years' War, and economic depression produced a steep demographic decline, particularly in southern Europe, central Europe, and the Ottoman Empire.

These periods of crisis were testing times for the major civilizations and the states that ruled them. Seemingly stable empires and kingdoms could be swept away. Strong migratory currents of people feeling devastation could change the ethnic and linguistic makeup of a region quite quickly. Major technological reversals could take place. For example, in the seventeenth and eighteenth centuries much of the Balkans reverted to seminomadic animal husbandry, whereas earlier there had been higher population densities and more widespread cultivation. The same thing had happened in parts of western Europe as a result of the Great Plague of the fourteenth century and the accompanying Hundred Years' War.

All the world's agrarian societies were subject to these kinds of cycles. We know that Mayan civilization in Central America went through some sort of political and ecological crisis and was in steep decay by the time the Europeans conquered this area in the sixteenth century. On the other hand, the Aztecs, farther to the north, were expanding at that time, as were the Incas in the Andes.

In the long run, those societies that learned to adapt to these catastrophes survived best. This often meant learning new agricultural techniques to overcome the problems of the past. There is no automatic correlation between catastrophe and innovation, because some societies simply fail to adapt. But ecological stress in agrarian societies is more likely to produce innovation than is a balanced ecological situation.

The first Chinese states were not based on rice cultivation, but over time the Chinese settled further south where wet rice cultivation was possible, and the southern regions became the key food-producing parts of the empire. Along with new production technologies, this required better transportation and the construction of a canal linking the south to the north so that rice could be transported northward. The Sui dynasty began this project in the late sixth century, but work on the canal system and many improvements continued for the next thousand years.

In about the ninth century the West Europeans discovered the use of the heavy plow, which allowed the heavy northern European soils to be turned over and provided much better drainage. Shortly afterwards, better ways of harnessing horses were discovered so that they could pull these heavier plows. This was the critical innovation that allowed the population of northern Europe to grow faster than that of southern Europe. It tipped the balance of power away from the Mediterranean. By the thirteenth century, there was a flourishing agrarian civilization in northwestern Europe based on this technology.

The heavy plow did not prevent the demographic cycle from occurring again during the fourteenth century, but at the time that the next such catastrophe hit Europe, northern Europe was taking another technological leap. First the Dutch and then the English discovered how to use clover as a crop that both replenished the soil and provided animal feed so that fields would not need to lie fallow for a time, as had been required before. This produced more animal power because clover and related crops provided good fodder. It enriched the fields and provided more fertilizer because clover adds nitrogen to the soil in which it is grown. These innovations set northwestern Europe, primarily the Dutch and English, on a course very different from that of other parts of Europe and allowed it to escape the general demographic and economic crisis that hit central and southern Europe and the eastern Mediterranean in the seventeenth century.

These illustrations are not meant to suggest that Chinese migrants into south China in the seventh century knew that they were trying to avoid the next ecological crisis, or that Dutch experiments with clover in the seventeenth century were anything other than short-range attempts to solve pressing problems. On the other hand, building government canals or inviting migrants who were known to possess superior technologies to populate the land were a part of deliberate, long-term strategies.

An example of the latter was the invitation by East European princes to German peasants to migrate into their lands and be guaranteed greater freedom and relief from taxes, just because it was known in the thirteenth century that German peasants understood the use of heavy plows and had access to better food-growing technologies. As late as the eighteenth century, the Russian state was inviting German migrants into its territories to create superior farming communities along the Volga River.

Whether by planning or accidentally, some agrarian societies made adaptations that allowed them eventually to start resisting the previously inevitable cycle of demographic and political decay. How and why this happened in western Europe, and the consequences, will be discussed in Chapter 3.

The Potential for Rapid Innovation: The Importance of Peripheries

It is difficult to explain why certain societies and cultures innovate more rapidly than others in the contemporary world. It is even harder to explain this for the past when we know much less about how innovation occurred.

It is not enough to say that ecological pressure or competition with other societies or internal turmoil produced change. That is true, of course, but sometimes instead of adaptive change there were changes that accelerated decline. In biological evolution, we know that the outcome of change is a matter of pure chance. Some mutations are useful and help an organism survive, and so make it more likely that its offspring will survive. To a considerable extent this is true of cultural evolution as well because humans have such a limited ability to predict the ultimate consequences of cultural, organizational, or technological change. Yet the parallel is not perfect because human beings are conscious of their acts and have the capacity to modify their behavior without having to wait for spontaneous mutations to occur.

We know that the transition to agriculture and states took place in unusually crowded places from which it was difficult to escape the problems of overcrowding. Aside from generating a perceived need to adapt, another advantage of crowding is that more ideas are exchanged simply because there are more people in contact with each other. In states, the priestly elite, whose business it was to think about the meaning of what was going on, became the first class of professional intellectuals who could devote a substantial portion of their lives to thinking and coming up with new ideas. It was also in the states of the Old World that writing was perfected to the point that interesting thoughts, stories, and speculations about how to run society, about the secrets of the natural world, and about the ultimate meaning of human life could be stored and passed on from generation to generation. This could freeze thought into old patterns, but at the same time it created the potential for progress in science and philosophy because the good ideas from the past were not just forgotten. It is not surprising, then, that many innovations in the early agrarian era came from the most densely populated, best organized, and most advanced state societies: the famous classical agrarian civilizations.

But coming up with new ideas or speculating about philosophy is not a sure guarantee of actual organizational or technological innovation. On the contrary, to every new idea there is resistance. Those who do not understand or do not want to change because new ways of doing things threaten their interests, or are afraid to question tradition for fear that this would bring society to ruin always exist, and not just in peasant villages.

Mancur Olson has worked out a general rule of social change that suggests that the longer there has been social stability, the more difficult it is to carry out reform. Established groups—economic classes, status groups, or groups with political power—consolidate their positions, learn to defend them, and resist innovation that might upset their interests. We see this in modern societies that become so blocked that no reforms are possible even if there is general recognition that they are needed. Ultimately, only catastrophe weakens established interest groups so much that resistance to innovation decreases, at least for a time, and rapid change can occur until new stability leads again to paralysis and stagnation.

We know that after a certain point in their histories some of the great agrarian civilizations lost the ability to innovate. Ancient Egypt was a notable case. Perhaps this was because of its relative security in the Nile valley and its isolation from the main trade and migration routes of the ancient eastern Mediterranean. Though conquered several times, it was less affected by external affairs than any of the other ancient Middle Eastern civilizations.

Relative isolation certainly decreases any given society's prospects for successful change. The Christian civilization of Abyssinia, later called Ethiopia, remained quite isolated in its highlands for many centuries and stagnated, so that it entered the twentieth century very far behind the more advanced parts of the Muslim world, let alone the Christian world to which it had originally been connected. Often only invasion and force applied from the outside changes an established civilization.

Another obstacle to change was that the elites of the great civilizations, both nobles and priests, possessed high status, that is, prestige. Not only their own people but their less advanced neighbors were awed by the great displays of wealth, the arts, the sciences, the temples, and all the various aspects of elite life in the great capitals of the major agrarian states. Even when these states became weak because of ecological, administrative, or political crises, their prestige and the memory of their greatness remained a model. It was common for tough barbarians from beyond the borders to break into established states and take them over. But though this might end the economic and political power of the old elites, it could not so easily eliminate their prestige.

Almost invariably barbarian invaders (and in the old centers of civilizations, all outsiders with less elaborate state structures and old cultures were "barbarians") adopted the ways of the elites they conquered and continued to respect many of their religious forms. Only if the outside conquerors were convinced of their own cultural superiority did this not take place.

Some of the most striking cases of the conversions that resulted from the continuing prestige of old elites are the repeated transformation of Mongol and Turkic nomads who invaded China and gradually became Sinicized themselves, often to the point of becoming absorbed by the culture they conquered and vanishing as separate groups. The Confucian literati who manned China's imperial administrations had such high prestige because of their learning that they remained models of proper behavior and virtue even for warrior nomads who commanded much greater force but wanted to emulate Chinese civilization.

Much the same happened in the late Roman Empire when the invading German barbarians adopted the version of Christianity that then prevailed in Rome. The Roman church, using Latin as its means of communication and in the beginning using high status Romans as its officials, kept its prestige even though it was often physically much weaker than the secular kingdoms that inherited power. In fact, Latin, the language of the Romans, retained its prestige as the main language of western European learning for almost fifteen centuries after the fall of Rome, as did the memory of Rome as an ideal for organizing political life. When the United States became independent in the late eighteenth century, it looked for models in histories of the ancient Roman Republic that had preceded the empire. When Napoleon became military dictator of the French Republic at the start of the nineteenth century, he turned to the Roman Empire as a model.

There are many other examples. The Turks who invaded the Muslim world previously dominated by Arabs and Persians in the tenth and eleventh centuries abandoned their tribal religions and became Muslims, and when the Mongols invaded the Middle East in the thirteenth and fourteenth century, they did the same. Arabic retained its prestige as the language of religion and Persian as a literary language even when neither Arabs nor Persians ruled the Middle East.

It is clear that there are stronger and weaker cultures. When Chinese invaders subdued southern peoples who were technologically less advanced, they Sinicized them; but when the Chinese were themselves invaded, they Sinicized their invaders, too. Nor is it simply a matter of technological superiority or the aura of an old civilization. Arabs swept out of the desert to conquer ancient Persia, but they quickly converted Persians to Islam. Islam and Christianity, as it happens, are extremely difficult to uproot, except through the expulsion or destruction of people. But they have the power to convert others. Perhaps it is because they carry with them a sense of such righteousness—certitude that they have the final answers to the question of why we exist and who we are. Ideas may be powerful by themselves.

Even so, the Arabs who invaded Persia in the seventh century and converted the Persians to their religions did not convert them to their way of life. It was the other way around. The Arab elites who conquered Persia became Persians with a Persian culture and style of government. Similarly, conquering Muslim Turks who destroyed the Byzantine Eastern Roman Empire in wars from the eleventh to the fifteenth century took over many of the forms of government and habits of the elite Greeks who had ruled the Byzantine Empire. Much of what we take to be traditional

Islamic culture—for example the subjection and isolation of women—is probably more Persian and Byzantine than something originally done by Arabs in the time of Muhammad.

What all this means is that once strong cultures take hold in agrarian societies, they develop an inherently conservative bias that slows down change, even when conquests occur. Thus, for example, the Sinicized Manchus who were ruling China in the nineteenth century clung to traditional Chinese Confucian behavior to resist modernizing their government. Repeated waves of invaders in India failed to upset the caste system that reduced the possibility of social mobility and innovation; rather, they succumbed to it, adding new layers of caste to Indian society.

There are so many examples of both change and resistance to innovation, of peoples who converted others to their culture and others who were themselves converted, that it is difficult to establish any general rules about how the process worked in agrarian societies. Nevertheless, by looking at a few exceptional cases of innovation, we can make some generalizations. One of the most interesting and important cases is that of the Greeks from about the sixth century B.C. until the first century B.C., when most of the Greek (and related Macedonian) states were conquered by Rome. In barely five centuries, the Greeks produced an astounding set of innovations.

Of all the ancient civilizations, the Greeks were the most self-conscious about their way of life. Their political philosophers did not take for granted, as their contemporaries in China and India did, that absolute monarchy was the best form of government. Rather, Plato, Xenophon, and Aristotle were only the most prominent Greek philosophers to examine the nature of tyrannies that prevailed in agrarian societies, and to try to find solutions for avoiding such governments. Thucydides studied war in an objective way and tried to find its causes. Greek theater and poetry examined human emotions with psychological insights that would not be matched again, except among some of the Romans who imitated them, for many centuries. The Greeks revolutionized sculpture and painting by being the first to make truly lifelike reproductions of the human form. The spread of Greek civilization throughout the eastern Mediterranean, Persia, and as far as parts of central Asia as a result of Alexander's conquest in the late fourth century B.C. produced what came to be known as Hellenistic culture. It thrived for about three more centuries. Its scientists and mathematicians discovered modern geometry, measured the size of the earth with extraordinary accuracy, developed notions of modern medicine, and improved a variety of technologies from sailing to mining.

Yet in many ways the Greeks were a marginal people until the time of Alexander the Great. They lived on the edge of a civilization that seemed much grander, that of the Persians. The Persian Empire went from the Aegean Sea to the Indus River and included Egypt, whereas the Greeks lived in small, competing city states who almost never managed to get together but fought constantly against each other. There was no uniform type of government. Some Greek cities were monarchies, other republics. Some were highly militaristic, and Sparta even made war the center of its entire existence. Some were primarily trading cities.

Spread around the Aegean, including what is now the coast of Turkey, the Black Sea, and in parts of southern Italy, Sicily, and even as far away southern France, most Greek states were actively engaged in exchanges— trade, exchange of ideas, wars, and political alliances—with their neighbors and other Greek states. It was this diversity, the unending competition, and the stimulus of the dangerous, enormous Persian giant next to them that probably produced such a marvelous explosion of innovation. It was not just the diversity of institutions that allowed the Greeks to compare and test what worked best, but also the existence, within the Greek world, of a common language and high culture that permitted these various little kingdoms and cities to exchange ideas with each other so fruitfully.

Much later, from about the tenth to the sixteenth century A.D., the diverse islands, trading kingdoms, and empires of Southeast Asia in what are today Indonesia and Malaysia experienced a similar situation. On the edge of two great civilizations, those of China and India, they were split into many competing units. As with the Greeks, many of them were used to long-distance, seaborne trade. The rich and innovative civilization that developed there might have become much like the earlier Greeks had it happened earlier and not been short-circuited by European conquest in the seventeenth century.

There are other examples. Venice, a trading city and port on the edge of the Byzantine Empire in the ninth and tenth century and a vital link between the eastern and western Mediterranean, was the first of the great Italian city states to start the revolution in trade, shipping, and politics that contributed so thoroughly to the Renaissance. The other great centers of that outburst of scientific, literary, and economic innovation from the thirteenth to the sixteenth century were also quarrelsome, independent city states fighting larger neighboring empires. They also shared a common language, if not a common form of government. Many were republics; some were hereditary dukedoms; some were petty tyrannies.

The capacity of little states at the edge of bigger, seemingly more solid empires to innovate is not at all rare. The Phoenicians, who were among the first to develop the modern European alphabet and were the greatest of the Mediterranean traders before the Greeks, also lived on the edge of bigger states in the Middle East. They also had several city states.

Islam came out of the Arabian desert, but it was not born in nomad tents. Rather, Muhammad was a merchant from an oasis merchant city that had many of the same functions as an island port in a sea crisscrossed by shipping lanes. And later, we will see that merchant cities on the edge of Western Europe—Antwerp, Amsterdam, and Lisbon—played similar innovative roles in early modern Europe.

When the Greek city states were overshadowed by the great Macedonian Empire of Alexander, the creativity of Greek civilization did not die, but it moved to some outlying areas. When later most of the Hellenistic world was conquered by Rome except for the eastern part, which became mostly Persian once again, Greek culture continued to be influential within Rome. But the rate of artistic and technological change slowed, and after the great conquests and consolidations of the first century and early second century A.D., the great Roman Empire ceased to make much progress.

In agrarian civilizations, then, somewhat marginal areas were more likely to be innovative and change than the heartlands of the great empires. Such areas were less likely to be blocked by established elites able to prevent change. The presence of many competing little political units was likely to stimulate change and adaptation more than the security of a single, big, united state. But the capacity to innovate was dependent on maintaining a fragile balance between competition on one hand and the chaos that would occur if warfare got out of hand and became too destructive on the other. At the opposite extreme, too great a success could lead to unification, which would produce its own deadening effect after several generations.

Perhaps most important of all is the fact that in the classical agrarian civilizations the most innovative and dynamic parts were not just little states on the edge of the civilization, but specifically merchant cities. Trade and commerce, generally considered inferior occupations in the high imperial cultures that ruled most of the agrarian world, were actually the greatest bearers of change and adaptation. In a sense it is as if trade, competition, and peripherality led to many more social and cultural "mutations" than the civilized heartlands, which worked to suppress change.

We will see in the next chapter that this was the key to the miraculous progress made by western Europe from the sixteenth to the twentieth century. Before going on to this theme, however, an important warning is necessary.

The Limits of Analogy: Societies Are Not Species, and Cultural Evolution Is Not Biological Evolution

Changes in cultures are not necessarily beneficial. New ways of organizing a society or some of its parts may produce failure rather than success. This is most obvious when one looks at the highly successful classical agrarian empires. All of them became increasingly involuted with time. Their administrative structures became larger but less efficient, they became drains on the economies that supported them, and they lost the flexibility to adapt to various emergencies. This was a matter of slowly drifting toward inefficiency. In the long run, such involution could make a big difference in decreasing adaptability. Rome was able to handle a number of barbarian invasions rather easily, but by the fifth century, it had lost its capacity to do this.

A civilization could regain its vigor, as China often did, by surmounting old problems with technological or organizational innovations. But mostly this occurred in response to previous catastrophes. In many mature agrarian civilizations adaptive innovations had to be brought in by peoples who had previously been peripheral to the central civilization.

It is easy to make an analogy between cultural changes in societies and genetic changes in organisms. In both cases, it is only after the fact, seeing what survived and what did not, that we can tell what was really most adaptive. In both cases, a wide variety of solutions may exist. And in both, failure to adapt leads eventually to death. But here the analogy between biological and cultural evolution breaks down.

Failure to adapt does not necessarily mean death for all the members of the society. Societies are neither individual organisms nor species. They are composed of many individuals who can adopt new ways even if their old culture fails. There are many cases in which whole social systems have failed and disappeared, but far fewer ones in which this has resulted in massive physical annihilation.

When a species is invaded by a competitor that takes over its niche in the ecology, it may well perish entirely. The same can happen if ecological conditions change. Only a small number of individuals with the right mutated traits manage to reproduce successfully, and their offspring eventually become a new species. But in human societies, languages and religions may change in a few generations, political systems can become quite different in a few years, and new technologies can come about almost as quickly without having the people who bore the old culture die out at all.

The error of confounding the extinction of species with the extinction of cultures has caused immense political problems in the twentieth century, and still does. It was because political interpretations of Darwin's theories led to this error that it became common in the late nineteenth and early twentieth century to believe that "fit" races would expand while "unfit" ones would die out. Aside from being a rationale for aggressive imperialism by Western states and Japan, it led to the error of identifying various human races, ethnic groups, and linguistic groups as virtually different "species" who competed with each other for the same ecological niche. Ultimately, too, it led to the idea that mixing "superior" and "inferior" races weakened the strong ones. But culture is not carried by genes, and all humans on earth are part of the same species. Thus the fact that there are stronger and weaker cultures, that some are more adaptable while some stagnate and are extinguished, has nothing at all to do with genetic differentiation, which takes place much too slowly to have a noticeable effect on how adaptable various cultures may be.

When the German tribes invaded and destroyed Rome, they did not physically exterminate the people they conquered, though of course the economic and political decline of the empire led to hardships, a higher death rate, and a diminution in population. The German conquerors established themselves as the overlords, mixed with the old Roman elite, and adopted their religion and language. Rome died, but the Romans did not, and even much of their culture survived in a new form.

When Arabs invaded and conquered Egypt, they gradually converted most of its inhabitants to Islam, and with time, all Egyptians came to speak Arabic. But the old Egyptians' descendants still live in Egypt. Some of them, perhaps 10 percent to 15 percent of the total, are Christians and use as their religious language a form of old Egyptian, Coptic. This does not mean that Muslim Egyptians are a different "race" that pushed out the old Egyptian "race." Egyptians are thoroughly mixed with Arab invaders, with Sudanese, with Turks, and with a variety of other eastern Mediterranean peoples, but the religious differences that exist between them are purely cultural and in no sense "racial."

The Chinese, who developed a remarkably uniform elite culture, are a mixture of many different peoples who were conquered by the original Chinese, or who conquered China and were absorbed.

Even the Japanese, who pride themselves on their racial purity, are a mixture of peoples. People related to the Polynesians probably migrated into Japan along the chain of islands from the Philippines to Taiwan and the Ryukyus. Others related to the Mongols, Manchurians, and Koreans came from the Asian mainland, probably through Korea. Still others, probably the oldest inhabitants of the Japanese islands, were like the Ainu, who still reside in the far north of Japan. Japanese culture is a mixture of all of these elements and a heavy dose of Chinese influence brought in primarily through contact with the Koreans. Both racial and cultural "purity" are constructed myths that raise great passion but have little to do with historical reality.

Much of the world still interprets "culture" as "biology." The term "cultural genocide" is popular among many intellectuals who fail to realize the implications of their reasoning. In fact, there is no such thing as "cultural genocide." Languages may change, religions may change, political systems may change, and technologies may change without "genocide" of any sort. No language spoken two thousand or even one thousand years ago would be understood by anyone today (except a few specialized scholars) even though modern languages are mutations of older ones, and even though the ways in which they have changed can often be traced through time. Similarly, no present culture is exactly the same as it was in the distant past, even though aspects of some cultures survived and others did not.

This is not to say that there were no cases in the past of wholesale killings and deportations. When the Mongols conquered the Tigris and Euphrates valley they destroyed the irrigation works that had sustained advanced civilizations for thousands of years, and up to 90 percent of the population died or had to move away. This area, now known as Iraq, never really recovered, at least not until the twentieth century. Nomads like the Mongols have had a similarly destructive effect elsewhere when they have turned agricultural lands, particularly irrigated ones in dry climates, into grazing lands.

Later, European settlers in America and Australia destroyed large numbers of people who were technologically much weaker than they were. A combination of brutality, the destruction of an ecological system to turn it into something else, and disease may actually cause the physical destruction of a whole society as well as the elimination of its culture. Yet generally this is not what happens when one culture replaces another. It certainly was not the rule when the elite of one society conquered and replaced the elite of another.

When Turkic nomads broke into the Anatolian heartland of the Byzantine Empire in the late eleventh century, they imposed their own Muslim culture on the area. Eventually, though not immediately, Greek speech and religion virtually vanished from central Anatolia (though it remained more common along the edges, near the Mediterranean coast, for a very long time). But the paintings on ceramics one sees from the Seljuk Turkish Empire of the twelfth century indicate that the Turks had Mongoloid features, like Turkic speakers to this day in central Asia. Today such features are rare in central Anatolia. Clearly, even though Greek is no longer spoken and there are no longer significant numbers of Christians there, the Turks intermingled with the Greeks and the many other peoples who inhabited Anatolia before them. Drastic cultural changes did not mean physical extermination of a whole people and their replacement by another, even though an old culture was ultimately replaced by a different one.

Even more striking was the later conquest of the Balkans by the Ottoman Turks. They neither replaced the Christian populations there nor even tried to convert them to Islam or to change their language. Ottoman rule, in fact, was neither particularly oppressive nor resented for several centuries until the Ottoman Empire itself degenerated into corruption and wasteful overtaxation.

Thousands of languages have died out—in fact, almost all languages ever spoken. This need not entail a calamity like the mass killings of the Jews by the Germans in the 1940s, or the expulsion and forced migration of Jews and Muslims by Spanish Christians from the late fifteenth to the seventeenth centuries, or the complete extermination of the Tasmanians by white settlers in the nineteenth century.

Unfortunately, in the twentieth century such murderous attempts to homogenize a culture, whether by outright murder or by forced expulsion, have become more common, not less common, than in the past. From the massacre of Armenians by the Turks during World War I (which was not at all the way the Turks had handled their relations with conquered peoples before the late nineteenth century), to the killing of the Jews by the Germans, to the massacres and forced migrations in India and Pakistan after independence, to the slaughter of Chinese, Chams, and Vietnamese by the Cambodians in the 1970s, to the "ethnic cleansing" in former Yugoslavia in the early 1990s, and with many other cases in between these, the incidence of such violent cultural clashes has been particularly high in the past one hundred years. On top of the political, religious, and ecological causes that produced some but not many such disasters in the past, there is now a sense that "culture" is so analogous to "race" that exterminating others only conforms to the supposed "law of nature."

To deny this does not mean that it is necessary to deny the utility of the analogy between cultural change and biological evolution. Certain cultural traits are more adaptive than others. There is no inherent virtue in any old habit, language, religion, or technology, and if these do not serve a society well, they will be replaced by more adaptive cultures from other societies. But that is where the analogy stops. Cultural survival is not a matter of competition to the death between competing cultures, or at least, it need not be. On the contrary, in the context of modern industrial societies cultural exchanges and the ability to learn from what others are doing should make cultural adaptation easier and more peaceful than ever before. Only by pushing a useful analogy much too far have some ideologies turned many cultural conflicts into such desperately murderous affairs.

Reference Notes
(Full references are in the bibliography)

Detailed studies of prestate people by anthropologists include classical studies by Napoleon Chagnon (*Yanomamö*), Paul Bohannan (*Justice and Judgment among the Tiv*), and Edmund Leach (*The Political Systems of Highland Burma*). A more literary, highly readable, excellent account of life in a prestate society is Peter Matthiessen's *Under the Mountain Wall*, about the stone age people of highland New Guinea. *African Political Systems*, edited by Fortes and Evans-Pritchard more than 50 years ago is still a wonderful collection contrasting different types of political institutions among prestate and early state peoples.

Claude Lévi-Strauss's *The Elementary Structures of Kinship* and Jack Goody's *The Oriental, the Ancient and the Primitive* are among the most useful studies of family structures in prestate and agrarian state societies.

An old but essential anthropological work by Bronislaw Malinowski, *Magic, Science and Religion*, explains the human drive to understand and master the external world and shows the similarities and differences in thinking about these subjects between different types of societies.

The premier synthetic work on the rise of states is Elman Service's *Origins of the State and Civilization*. The nature of power in early states has been discussed by Michael Mann in his first volume of *The Sources of Social Power*.

There are so many fascinating accounts of the classical agrarian civilizations that it seems unjust to have to pick just a few to cite and recommend. On ancient Greece the work of Moses Finley stands out, and his edited work *The Legacy of Greece* contains good essays on the most important aspects of Greece's long-run influence. Trigger, Kemp, O'Connor, and Lloyd have assembled a rather dry but solid and up-to-date explanation of what we know about ancient Egypt in their collective book called *Ancient Egypt*. Mark Elvin's *The Pattern of the Chinese Past* remains controversial among specialists, but it offers one of the most cogent explanations for both China's greatness and its eventual stagnation. Marshall Hodgson's three-volume *The Venture of Islam* is a definitive study of the Islamic civilizations from their beginnings in Arabia through their periods of greatness and decline. Marc Bloch's *Feudal Society*, based on his research in the 1920s and 1930s, is still the most readable comprehensive work on the nature of European feudal society, though some of its interpretations have been questioned by later scholars.

Colin McEvedy, who has published a series of superb historical atlases with narrative commentary, including ones about African, American, medieval, and modern history, also has one called *The Penguin Atlas of Ancient History*. No other brief work gives a beginner as good a sense of the rise and fall of states and civilizations in ancient North Africa, Europe, and the Near East, including the northwestern parts of India.

The harshness of life in agrarian times is partly captured by the work of Marvin Harris cited at the end of Chapter 1, but also by William McNeill's provocative, path-breaking study of the great plagues that swept through the civilized world during the agrarian age, *Plagues and People*. Though quite different, Louis Dumont's study of caste in India, *Homo Hierarchicus*, lays out the consequences of extreme inequality in agrarian societies. James Scott's *The Moral Economy of the Peasant* provides superb insights of how peasants always surviving on the margin of disaster actually live and think about the world, and what occasionally drives them to desperate rebellion.

William McNeill's sweeping study of war, *The Pursuit of Power*, is vital for those who would like to understand the connection between civilization, progress, and organized violence. Paul Kennedy's best-selling *The Rise and Fall of Great Powers* argues that both agrarian and modern industrial great powers inevitably overextend themselves and thus bring about their own fall by spending too much on their military.

The fall of various great empires because of ecological crisis, nomadic invasions, internal social conflict, and economic crisis is examined by the essays assembled in Carlo Cipolla's edited *The Economic Decline of Empires*. Jack Goldstone's new *Revolution and Rebellion in the Early Modern World* specifically addresses the connection between demographic pressures and rebellion in agrarian empires.

Probably no one has approached the scope of Max Weber's sweeping analysis of how agrarian civilizations operate, and why some progressed while others did not. Though his *Economy and Society* is long, often repetitive, and based on research that is now more than a century old, selected parts should still be consulted to understand the dilemmas faced by agrarian states trying to administer themselves. Weber is also excellent in explaining the rise of capitalism in Europe.

Mancur Olson's *The Rise and Decline of Nations* is meant to apply more to modern than to agrarian societies, but it presents a convincing general theory of why success and peace bring eventual social paralysis and eventual disaster to all societies by blocking further evolution.

3

The Rise of the West

Although agrarian civilizations can have highly stable patterns of social and cultural organization over many centuries, it would be entirely wrong to conclude that they were immune to change. Some important types of technological, political, and religious adaptation were outlined in the preceding chapter. Compared to the rate of cultural change in prestate societies, the changes between about 3500 B.C. and 1500 A.D. occurred very quickly. In those five thousand years writing, statecraft, advanced metallurgy, complex architecture, plow agriculture, great religions, and all other aspects of what we call "civilization" were invented, whereas before it had taken tens of thousands of years for major change to occur. But compared to the five thousand years that ended in about 1500, what followed witnessed change so massive and rapid that it makes the first five millennia of civilized life seem almost stagnant.

We know a lot about changes after 1500 A.D.; however, the creation of the modern world is a subject that is controversial and undergoing continual revision by contemporary scholars. Before embarking on an explanation of how it was that one agrarian civilization, and a somewhat marginal one at that, transformed the entire world and briefly took it over, a few of these controversies should be mentioned.

It is now the fashion to dismiss western Europe's accomplishments for two reasons. First, there is a tendency to blame Europeans for all the ills of the world. In a sense, of course, this is justified because it was in a part of western Europe that the modern world was invented, and it was from there that modernity was spread around the world. Much of what anyone may dislike about the modern world has its origin in western Europe. But it is important to remember what was replaced by modernization. Europeans did not invent war, the overuse of resources, social inequality, slavery, dishonesty, cruelty, or greed. They merely found ways to become more efficient at using their resources and learned to control their environment better than other cultures. Their discoveries have allowed humans to live longer, to reproduce more successfully, and ultimately, because of this material success and the greater freedom from want that it makes possible, to escape from the bonds of agrarian society in which most humans were entrapped for five thousand years. We should remember that what the Europeans discovered was a way to escape from social systems in which more than 90 percent of the population consisted of virtual slaves or serfs, in which disease was endemic, and in which almost no one, except for a tiny number of elite individuals, had much freedom at all.

In the process of doing this, Europeans also destroyed the remaining prestate and preagrarian societies that existed. But by 1500 these were already marginal and on the way to being extinguished by the more numerous, more technologically sophisticated agrarian states that already included the overwhelming majority of the human population.

The second broad reason for dismissing the change wrought by Europeans is to say that Europe only represents a small portion of the human population, and that to emphasize only what happened there is to neglect the accomplishments of the others. Again, there is a certain obvious truth to this. No civilization has been particularly good at recognizing the merits of others. The Chinese, the Muslims, the ancient Egyptians, the Romans, and the Aztecs all considered themselves superior to the peoples with whom they came into contact. Within their own spheres—East Asia, the Middle East, northeastern Africa, and Mexico—these peoples created dominant cultures that transformed others around them. The Europeans merely did this on a far larger scale than anyone before them. Yet, like older great civilizations, the Europeans also absorbed much from those with whom they came into contact, often quite unconsciously. And the people they transformed did not just become copies of the Europeans. They adapted their cultures to European influences.

But even after taking these criticisms into account, it would be an evasion of the most important historical fact of the last five hundred years to pretend that Europe did not create an entirely new, industrialized, urbanized, and much more highly populated world than that which existed during the long agrarian stage of civilization. In the modern world it is possible to adapt to that fact, to take from European civilization what made it so dynamic, and to prosper as have the Europeans. Or it is possible to fail to adapt and to remain mired in poverty and weakness. Rejecting the changes wrought by Europe, that is, rejecting modernity, is as futile as wishing that agrarian societies had not replaced gathering and hunting ones.

This does not mean that the descendants of the people who invented modern, postagrarian civilization are necessarily the ones who will succeed best with it in the very long run. There have been many examples in the past of societies who adopted some aspects of a great civilization and brought it to greater heights than its originators. Christian Europe in the Middle Ages and the early modern period was peopled not by the descendants of those who invented Christianity, but by the descendants of others who converted and who made more of the idea than its originators. Islamic civilization has long been something much more than the possession of the descendants of Muhammad's followers from central Arabia. Chinese culture imported and modified into Japan resulted in something quite different and in some ways more adaptable than the original. So it may be with Europe's modern, industrial civilization. For example, an adapted form of it in East Asia may soon prove to be more successful even than the original. Culture, as we know, is not a genetic property but may be learned, adapted, and improved by others, while the originators of certain ideas may fail to utilize them fully.

Europe's Ecological Advantages

Any observer able to travel around the world in the year 1000 would not have concluded that western Europe was destined for world dominance. China was far more advanced in science and technology, its cities were incomparably bigger and more sophisticated, its level of literacy was higher, its statecraft was more efficient, and it was a far bigger and more unified society than the fractured, quarrelsome, feudal, and entirely rural little western European states. The Muslim world contained a number of states that were in every respect more advanced than the western Europeans, including the Umayyad Caliphate in Spain, the Fatimid Caliphate in northern Africa, Sicily, Palestine, and Syria, and several Persian emirates to the east. The greatest Christian state was not in western Europe at all, but was the Eastern Orthodox, Greek-speaking Byzantine Empire centered on its capital, Constantinople, one of the greatest cities in the world at that time. Up to 80 percent of western Europe, in contrast, was still covered by huge, wild forests.

In the year 1000, western Europe, not including Muslim Iberia, had no more than twenty million people, while China had some eighty million living in a unified empire under the rule of the Song dynasty. About 6 or 7 percent of China's population lived in cities of over one hundred thousand people, and the capital, Kaifeng, had well over a half million people. The only Christian West European city at that time to have as many as twenty thousand people was Venice, and it lived by trading with the Muslims and Byzantines. The Muslim world at that time had almost twenty cities larger than Venice, and Constantinople was at least ten times bigger. Paris and London were tiny towns, and even Rome, which had about a half million people at the height of the Roman Empire, probably had no more than about ten thousand people.

What happened between 1000 and 1500 that allowed western Europe to set out on the conquest of the world? Why, between 1500 and 1800, did its science and technology develop so quickly that they prepared the way for rapid industrialization and urbanization?

Whereas the earliest civilizations and states developed in constricted river valleys, and these areas remained the centers of civilization for a long time after that, once they were filled with people they were subject to great catastrophes. Irrigation works had to be maintained. Nomadic raiders in surrounding dry regions had to be fought off. When these great river valleys, such as the Nile, the Tigris-Euphrates, and the Yellow River, were united by a powerful empire, their capacity to support large numbers of people and great cities made them great powers. But when their social and political systems broke down, so did their economies, and it could take centuries to recover because their capital, their means of production, was destroyed. Irrigation works had to be rebuilt; animal stocks that were essential for plowing, food, and transportation had to be brought back to their previous levels; and the human population had to recover.

This problem was most severe in the Middle East because it is so dry. Egypt, for example, reached a population of some three million in about 1300 B.C. and a maximum of some five million when it was the heart of the Fatimid Caliphate in the year 1000 A.D., but it only had between three and four million people in 1800 A.D. During these three thousand years the population rose and fell in periodic cycles that marked repeated catastrophes and slow recoveries. The area of Mesopotamia (modern Iraq), which had up to two million inhabitants during the Assyrian Empire in about 700 B.C. and perhaps slightly more than that in the year 1000 A.D., had no more than one million in 1800. In other words, in the greatest centers of the ancient Middle East, the very areas that also became the centers of Islamic civilization, ecological circumstances, the interplay between the physical geography and human action, led to frequent disasters that hindered growth and obliged the inhabitants to rebuild repeatedly in order to return to previous levels of well-being.

China, India, and most of the Mediterranean avoided the extreme problems of Egypt and Mesopotamia because population could spread out from the original centers of civilization. But all of them were equally subjected to periods of extreme drought, to invasions by marauding nomads and conquerors, and to severe cycles of prosperity and collapse. Most of the regions bordering the Mediterranean were particularly subject to ecological failure because overcropping and grazing can easily destroy the ecological balance. North Africa, for example, was one of the main granaries of the Roman Empire, but later, due to invasions by nomadic Arabs whose herds badly overgrazed it, it fell into decline in the eleventh century.

The climate of western Europe is quite different. Rainfall is evenly distributed throughout the year. Extreme periods of dryness and flooding are rare. Complex irrigation systems did not need to be maintained, so the economy was much less dependent on effective political rule to maintain prosperity. There are no adjacent dry zones with nomads. This meant that major disruptions were far less common than in the other major civilized regions of the world. Once stocks of animals had been built up and agricultural improvements made, this capital was more likely to survive and continue to grow instead of having to be replaced periodically. Indeed, from some time in the Middle Ages on, the slow accumulation of capital in western Europe raised productivity to the highest levels in the world. That is, for every unit of human labor, it became possible to produce more food than in other regions.

Western Europe north of the Mediterranean remained a marginal part of the civilized world until the superior, deep plows developed after the ninth century made it possible to exploit the moist, heavy soils that had been covered by forest. But after about the year 950 there was a period of almost uninterrupted expansion of agriculture, trade, and population growth in western Europe for four hundred years. Then there was a setback with the bubonic plague, but even this did not destroy animal stocks or reverse agricultural improvements, and growth resumed within a century. This is what tipped the balance in power between western Europe and the Mediterranean and Muslim Middle East.

But that is not a sufficient explanation for what happened to western Europe, because, after all, in China there was also a long period of agricultural growth and the clearing of new lands (in the south), a vast expansion of population and trade, and important technological improvements. China remained the most advanced part of the world until the sixteenth century.

It was China's very success that ultimately slowed change. If instead of comparing western Europe to all of the major civilizations we compare it only to China, we immediately see a startling difference. Because Europe was geographically split into many small river valleys, it was very difficult to unify it. In China, control of the Yellow River valley, and later of the Yangzi River valley, was sufficient to give a state control over all of China. Because it was easier to maintain control over one or two valleys and to use their rivers as means of communication, China developed a far greater unity than Europe. From this, there developed a strong bureaucratic administrative system in China. This did not happen in Europe, even though the Roman Christian Church certainly tried to create such an administration. But Europe never had a real parallel to the corps of Confucian officials in China. It remained split into many competing kingdoms, principalities, and cities.

Western Europe in the Middle Ages reproduced on a larger scale the much earlier Greek situation: It was a divided, quarrelsome civilization somewhat marginal to the really great centers of power. And yet, through the Western Christian Church and Latin, it possessed a way for its thinkers, priests, and merchants to communicate with each other and exchange ideas and goods.

That brings us a bit closer to an explanation. Western Europe, once its farmers learned to handle heavy, moist soils, had ecological advantages that most other civilized regions lacked. And it was not politically united, thus fostering greater internal competition.

Religious Discordance and Political Stalemate: The Basis for Western Rationalization

Throughout the Middle Ages—that is, between the fall of the Western Roman Empire in the late fifth century until the late fifteenth century—the political disunity of Europe presented its thinkers with a severe problem. Being Christian, they expected a concordance between their religious beliefs and the condition of the world. Unlike the resignation and acceptance of endless, repetitive cycles that was part of Hinduism, or the social ethic of Confucianism, which accorded well with the success of the Chinese imperial state, Christian beliefs in western Europe were radically at variance with the persisting reality of disunity. There was a pope and a religious bureaucracy he headed, but it was in frequent conflict with secular authorities who were themselves always at war with each other. This endless war and disorder did not prevent the economy and society from growing, as such conditions did in the ecologically more fragile Islamic Middle East, but the longer these conditions persisted, the greater the anomaly between what was expected and what was happening. Christianity, as we saw earlier, is like Islam in believing that history has a purpose, to manifest the single God's will and drive toward universal perfection.

In fact the political situation in western Europe grew ever more confusing. Competition between feudal lords and centralizing kings persisted throughout the Middle Ages, and though some kings, notably in France and England, managed to create more centralized administrations, they were never able to bring their nobles under complete control. In other parts of Europe, particularly in Germany and Italy, regional lords and trading cities broke the power of centralized monarchs and further fragmented the political structure. Everywhere, the Church was yet another political actor, siding sometimes with kings, sometimes with lords, sometimes with increasingly independent towns prospering from the revival of trade after the tenth century.

One of the main consequences of this fragmentation was that merchant cities in Europe were able to bargain for considerable freedom and self-government. In contrast, in the Middle East they were subjected to control by mercenary military force, and in China they could never escape control by the empire.

Merchants and town artisans everywhere in the world have a peculiar outlook on life. Unlike warrior nobles, whose chief goal is to be brave and honorable, or peasants, who fall back on resignation and magic to help them out of difficult situations, those whose life consists of commerce are careful calculators who come to believe that it is possible to understand the environment as one understands doing one's job: by measuring what resources and investments one makes and by carefully maximizing profits. The lives of merchants and urban artisans are dominated by ledgers and accounts, not by the search for honor and the glory of battle, nor by attempts to magically manipulate an uncontrollable natural environment.

Rationality, that is, an attitude that it is possible to calculate and purposively manipulate the environment, is more likely to be developed in an urban than in a rural setting because urban life is less subject to the vagaries of nature. It is more likely to grow among peaceful merchants than among warriors, who must depend far more on luck to survive and whose lives are more dependent on developing physical than intellectual skills.

The political stalemate in western Europe between kings, lords, and the church allowed a more rational urban culture to thrive and establish itself. At the same time, the discordance between the reality of a divided Europe and the perception that there should be more harmony led intellectuals to reexamine Christian beliefs. The mixture of a growing, rational urban culture and the attempt to harmonize religious teachings with reality produced a rationalizing religious outlook. Its basic assumption was that the universe must make more sense than it seemed to, and that if one searched hard enough, it should become possible to find the calculable laws according to which everything worked.

This deep belief that the laws of God must manifest themselves as a set of regular, calculable relationships and that these were subject to rational understanding was not unique to western Europe. Urban dwellers and troubled philosophers had thought along these lines in all civilizations. But it was only in western Europe that there were enough individuals thinking this way, and for a long enough period of time, for this new way of viewing the world to gain a firm foothold. For this to happen, it was important that no unified imperial structure bring Europe together.

In agrarian societies rationalizing thinkers are inherently dangerous. They question the legitimacy of hereditary monarchs because they examine the political system from the point of view of practicality and efficiency. Their intellectualism demeans warriors and the ethic of noble honor, which is based on action rather than thought. They bring into doubt the great religions of resignation, which are supposed to keep the peasantry satisfied with their miserable lot, because they suggest that improvement is possible and that human beings have the capacity to make their own decisions. They cast doubt on established religious thinking by subjecting theology to its own rationality, that is, to testing and questioning in order to find the truth, as opposed to simply receiving it as it has been handed down over the ages. In all agrarian societies the really daring rationalist thinkers have been accused of being heretics and of being a menace to the established order in society. They might be protected by an occasionally enlightened prince, but they were more likely to wind up being imprisoned or killed by irate authorities.

Part of the European advantage was that such thought was somewhat protected by the diversity of political power and by the towns' interests in maintaining their freedom. Only in an independent urban environment were there many who might agree with dangerously rational thinkers. Only where it was possible for a thinker to flee to a safe haven could the continuing development of rational thought take place. Thus both political division and powerful towns were necessary.

Through a set of coincidences, western Europe, like ancient Greece before it, and for many of the same reasons, developed a greater tradition of free thought and rationality than other agrarian civilizations. And at the same time, it was thriving because of its growing agriculture and commerce. Had western Europe been a united imperial state like China, there would not have been such an impetus to engage in religious self-examination. Had there not been such a political stalemate that allowed towns independence and pitted church, kings, and nobles against each other, there would not have been as much space for the development of rational thought.

Science, Knowledge, and Exploration in China and Western Europe

Throughout the European Middle Ages, from about 500 A.D. to 1500 A.D., China was technologically more advanced. This is where printing, gunpowder, the compass, and many other technologies were invented.

From the tenth to the fourteenth centuries in China there were major advances in mathematics, theoretical science, and medicine. But this was based entirely on central government support. The political turmoil that accompanied the Mongol conquest in the thirteenth century, and even more the civil wars and plagues that beset China in the fourteenth century when the Mongols were expelled, destroyed the basis for that support. The Chinese dynasty that inherited power after the Mongols, the Ming, were cultural conservatives who emphasized received Confucian virtues rather than science, and some of the mathematical discoveries of the previous centuries were forgotten. The examination system, which entailed enormous amounts of time spent memorizing the commentaries on Confucian thought, absorbed the energies of China's intellectuals since this was now the only way to move into the bureaucratic elite.

During the fifteenth century the Chinese sailed around Southeast Asia into the Indian Ocean. They visited India, the eastern coast of Africa, and Arabia, and their ships were much larger than anything the Europeans possessed. But these activities were considered dangerous by the imperial court and bureaucracy because they would lead to the enrichment of merchants, who would benefit from long-distance trade, and of the port cities of Quangdong (what Westerners call the province of Canton). The government prohibited the construction of big oceangoing ships on the pretext that this would discourage piracy. The empire was strong enough to impose its wish, and exploration stopped.

At the end of the same century, the Portuguese sailed around western Africa into the Indian Ocean and opened trade routes between Europe, India, and Southeast Asia. This was the beginning of the European domination of the world. The Chinese had been there first, but deliberately renounced expansion in order to conserve their old social order.

The experience of the West was quite different. The search for rational explanations furthered both mathematical thinking and the compulsion to verify scientific laws through experimentation. It was the combination of these two in the mercantile Renaissance cities of northern Italy in the fifteenth and sixteenth centuries that created modern West European science. Yet Galileo, the greatest scientific thinker of the early seventeenth century, had his work proscribed by the Catholic Church because it threatened old, established religious beliefs. Because the Church was so powerful, and because during the sixteenth century most of Italy came under the control of the Hapsburg Empire that was trying to unify Europe and impose the same kind of conservative culture as that which the Ming had successfully imposed on China, Italy lost its place as the most innovative part of Europe. But in northern Europe, especially in the merchant cities of the Netherlands and in England, Protestants defeated the Catholic Church and beat off the Hapsburg armies. It was in the Netherlands and England that European science continued to thrive, and it was these Protestant trading nations that became the great innovators of the seventeenth and eighteenth centuries.

Had there been a region of China on its periphery able to take advantage of the best of Chinese culture while remaining independent of the conservative imperial court and bureaucracy, it is very likely that it would have been the first part of the world to discover modern science and technology. But in China there was no such place.

On the whole it was the religiously deviant in western Europe, not just Protestants, but Puritan Protestants, who pushed rationalization the furthest. They felt compelled to prove their belief. The greatest of the Puritan Protestant scientists in England in the late seventeenth and early eighteenth century was Newton, who virtually invented modern physics and calculus. Had Newton been living in Italy at that time, his work would have been banned, and like Galileo, he would have been arrested, or worse.

Protestantism was actually strongest in the merchant cities of northern Europe and in societies that had the most commercialized economies. This led Max Weber, an early twentieth-century German sociologist, to conclude that Protestantism was causally related to the invention of modern capitalism. Indeed it was, but the relationship between capitalism and Protestantism was reciprocal. That is, it was among urban capitalists that Protestantism developed furthest because these were the people most eager to apply the same calculating rationality and ethic of individual responsibility to their faith that they used in their work.

The development of Western science was not based on the lucky accident of an occasional king who supported research and philosophical thinking, much less on the birth of a few geniuses like Galileo or Newton. It was part of a more broadly based movement that could only have occurred in a civilization with a secure and growing urban merchant tradition, with enormous religious doubt, and with a multiplicity of political units and classes fighting with each other for supremacy. Had the Catholic Church been able to repress Protestant heresy, had the Hapsburg emperors managed to conquer all of Europe as they almost did in the sixteenth century, or had a great ecological catastrophe destroyed the economic basis of Europe's prosperity between 1500 and 1700, it is unlikely that western Europe, particularly its northwestern portion, would have established a new, more rational type of culture.

The same conclusion can be drawn from the success of the European explorations that began in the late fifteenth century and eventually spread European trade and power throughout the world. At first it was the somewhat marginal Portuguese who led the way. When Spain became the main colonizer of the New World, however, it used its new power and the precious metals it derived from the Americas to try to create a unified European Empire. It was there that the Hapsburgs based themselves in the sixteenth century. But Spain ruined itself in the process, killing both its commerce and free thinkers by overtaxing the economy and by imposing rigid thought control on its intellectuals in order to maintain Catholic doctrine. The more marginal Dutch and English, who seemed to have far less power than mighty Spain, inherited most of the trade and advantages of the Spaniards and Portuguese and pushed exploration further.

There was, in fact, a close connection between the impulse to explore new lands and the search for scientific laws. It was more than just the search for profits and power that drove the Europeans to explore, though both of these played a role. It was also the need to know. And it was ultimately because of the knowledge accumulated about other peoples, other cultures, other climates, and geography in general that Europeans became the first to develop the systematic comparative study of history and politics on a large scale. In the late seventeenth century and in the eighteenth, this led to the Enlightenment. During the Enlightenment political philosophers, primarily in France and England, developed notions about individual liberty and constitutional, representative government that became the basis for modern Western democracy.

It is impossible to separate commerce, the urge for individual advancement, scientific curiosity, and progress. Newton, for example, was supported by the government of England because merchants sailing the oceans of the world wanted better methods of measuring their position from the stars. This very practical concern was furthered by advances in astronomy, and it was with these that Newton was able to formulate his theory of how gravity worked.

The depredations of Europeans seeking precious metals or African slaves to work the sugar plantations of the new world also led to contacts with strange new societies. From such ignoble beginnings came the first philosophical speculations about the true nature of humanity, and from the world's main trading nation, England, came the modern world's first movement to abolish slavery in the eighteenth century.

The progress made by Europe from the Renaissance to the Enlightenment was a function not of any inherent superiority among Europeans, but of a different structure of opportunity. There was more room for and more reward for independent thinkers, just as there was more leeway for commerce and independent urban life than in the other civilizations of the world. Rationality was more valued. Science and a new kind of philosophical speculation took root. To be sure, all this happened only among a tiny minority of intellectuals, but they were tolerated, respected, and allowed to continue their work in a few parts of Europe. That was enough to change the world.

The Growth of European Empires and the Transformation of the Economy

The rationalization of scientific and religious thought did not immediately produce major technological or economic changes. But it was part of a general spirit of innovation that resulted in countless technical improvements. Mining, manufacturing, medicine, book printing, painting, literature, architecture, agriculture, and many other aspects of the material and expressive culture of Europe were changed. Legal and administrative systems were rationalized and improved, allowing states to extract greater revenues and build bigger, stronger armies and navies.

As far as the rest of the world was concerned, however, the most dramatic aspect of the change in Europe was its rapid expansion around the globe. This was due to improved shipbuilding, better navigation techniques, and the development of effective naval artillery and portable musketry. With these tools, the Spaniards invaded America in 1492, and within fifty years they had control of a vast stretch of territory from Mexico to Chile. The Portuguese used superior naval skills to seize control of the commerce of the Indian Ocean, and they set up a series of trading ports that went from Lisbon all the way to Macau in China.

The Spanish and Portuguese empires were only first steps, however. In the seventeenth century the Dutch seized control of the Portuguese trading routes and established themselves in the East Indies (what is now Indonesia), along the coast of China, and as far away as Japan with which they opened trade routes. The Dutch, English, and French took over many of the Caribbean islands from Spain and established sugar plantations. It was in order to find workers for these plantations that the Europeans began to trade their goods for slaves with coastal African kingdoms.

The impulse to colonize and profit from trade, along with continual improvements in the technology of sailing and of firearms, meant that the spectacular expansion of the sixteenth and seventeenth century was followed by even deeper penetration. It was only in the eighteenth and early nineteenth centuries that the Europeans perfected their ships and weapons sufficiently to be able to take on the most powerful continental civilizations of Asia and to send large numbers of colonists overseas, mostly to the Americas. India was fought over by the French and English, and after the English won in 1763, they quickly seized most of the rest of India in the next half century. China was forced to cede ports and trading concessions in the mid-nineteenth century. North America was populated by European immigrants. In the late nineteenth century the Europeans found ways of combating malaria and moved from the coastal parts of Africa they had long controlled into the interior. By 1900 West Europeans directly or indirectly controlled most of the world.

The vast expansion of trade that occurred as a result of the European expansion spurred economic development within western Europe as well. Cities grew and needed more food, so agricultural markets developed and spurred technological improvements. We have already seen that in the seventeenth and eighteenth centuries the Dutch and English pioneered an agricultural revolution by growing fodder crops to replenish the soil and provide more animal feed. This allowed better plowing and, for those who could invest in improvements of the land, greater profits. Old village communities with set habits and conservative production techniques were forced to give up their lands to innovative landowners more interested in making money than in preserving old social forms.

Money and the ability to profit from trade and production became more important than simply possessing noble blood or ancient titles. This happened first in the Netherlands and England but then spread elsewhere in western Europe. Though both traditional village communities and the old nobility resented these changes and considered them to be disturbing signs of greed and disregard for ancient virtues, it was this commercialization of the economy that did more than anything to consolidate the rationalizing, mercantile, urban ethic of western Europe and make it unassailable.

In the late eighteenth century, vast new opportunities for profit, the growth of global trading, and the technological improvements that had occurred combined in what was then the world's foremost trading and commercial society, Great Britain (that is, the united states of England, Wales, Scotland, and Ireland) to produce a virtual revolution in production. This is what came to be called the Industrial Revolution, and we will discuss it in the next chapter.

Overcoming the Agrarian Population Cycle

As late as the seventeenth century much of western Europe went through another of the demographic cycles that had beset agrarian societies for thousands of years. Disease and war decimated Germany and large areas around the Mediterranean. Population declined. But in the northwestern parts of the continent, those areas that had already absorbed the greatest technological changes, the decline was insignificant. This was the last time western Europe was subjected to such a cyclical decline. In modern, industrial societies there may be wars and destruction, there may be depressions and suffering, but technology always allows production of essentials to accelerate faster than population growth. This is one of the defining characteristics of the new age that Europe invented. The benefits of better food-growing technology, better transportation to carry food to those areas suffering temporary shortages, and eventually the control of epidemic diseases spread throughout the world and caused an unprecedented population explosion. This was mostly due to the sharp fall in infantile death rates due to better nutrition that began in Europe.

From 1500 to 1900, Europe's population went up about five times, from about 80 million to almost 400 million. But England's population went up almost nine times during this period. Later, especially in the twentieth century, the rate of population slowed drastically in the richest countries because people began to want fewer children, while the same benefits of what had boosted population earlier in Europe spread and

TABLE 3-1

Approximate World Population by Area, in Millions

Year	Europe	America	Africa[a]	Middle East[b]	South Asia[c]	East Asia
1500	80	15	40	30	125	130
1700	105	10	50	30	190	200
1800	180	25	60	35	225	370
1900	390	150	100	55	375	530
2000	700	800	700	350	1700	1450

a. Excluding North Africa.
b. Including North Africa.
c. Including Indian subcontinent and Southeast Asia.

caused enormous population growth even in the poorest part of the world (see Table 3-1).

Different eras of social and cultural evolution are marked by sharp discontinuities in the rates of change. Just as the invention of agriculture and the state irrevocably altered social life, so did the invention of modern, industrial society. And in all of these cases, a good measure of the discontinuity was that all of a sudden the population began to grow much more quickly than before.

We know what the ultimate consequences of the invention of agriculture and states turned out to be. But we are very far from knowing what will be the final results of the very recent changes that have propelled us into an entirely new era.

The Invention of Nationalism and Its Consequences

The invention of cheap, mass printing spread literacy. This was particularly true in the Protestant societies of northern Europe because there people were supposed to be able to read the Bible and think about God on their own. It was in England that growing literacy and commercialization of the economy led to the beginnings of modern nationalism. In other states there had been a sense of pride and solidarity among the elite, but rarely did it extend far beyond the privileged few in agrarian societies. Even in China, which certainly had the most developed sense of cultural unity of any large agrarian state, this was a matter of elite perception. But in England in the sixteenth and increasingly the seventeenth and eighteenth centuries, the majority of the population was brought into the nation. The same occurred in France in the eighteenth century.

Until the development of modern nationalism most people who were not in the elite identified themselves by their family or clan, by their village, and by their religion. This meant that they had a vague loyalty to those with whom they shared their faith and a greater sense of belonging to those who lived immediately around them or who were directly related. But the state as such commanded little loyalty. It consisted of a distant government that taxed as much as it could and rendered few if any concrete services in return.

The idea of the modern nation as developed first in England and then in France was quite different. The nation as an ideal replaced other forms of political loyalty and allowed the state to call on the emotional as well as the fiscal support of its citizens. Whereas most armies in agrarian states had consisted of professional soldiers and paid mercenaries, it now became possible to draft men into the army, and increasingly, to expect loyal service from them. The first large-scale call to arms by a modern army occurred in France during its revolutionary wars from the early 1790s to 1815.

In return for this new and higher loyalty, citizens came to expect that their state would render more services than in the past. This coincided well with Enlightenment political philosophy, which saw states as compacts between people and their rulers. Old-fashioned states in which the powerful used their power to exploit the masses came to be seen as illegitimate.

This new conception of government changed social life as greatly as the technological improvements and increasing commerce that were causing economic change. As the idea of nationalism spread, people came to be much more integrated with their governments than before and much more passionate about the competition between states. In the modern world most people identify themselves first of all as citizens of a state, and they expect that this will confer certain privileges as well as obligations upon them.

But nationalism quickly turned into a dangerous weapon. It allowed certain states to mobilize greater energies for fighting their wars, but it also produced counternationalism among the more backward societies that saw their independence endangered by the most successful new nations of western Europe, England, and France. Having before them the example of these successful new nation-states, kings and emperors in neighboring states tried to foster the same sentiments among their people and to play on the resentments aroused by the greater political successes of the most powerful western European states.

The new nationalism in England and France was essentially democratic, as it was in England's offshoot, the United States. All of the people were supposed to participate in government, to owe allegiance to the nation, and to benefit from being in it. England and the United States had old parliamentary traditions on which to base their new democratic ideals, but the French did not. This was the primary cause of the French Revolution, which first established a parliamentary democracy and then became a nationalist military dictatorship under the rule of Napoleon. Napoleon used French nationalism and the enthusiasm it aroused to mobilize giant armies that came close to conquering all of Europe. It was the example of France that stimulated German nationalism, and the successful German example that spread the sentiment further into central and eastern Europe. Similarly, it was the colonial conquests by the French and English, and later by the other Europeans, that taught people around the world the idea of nationalism and democracy.

Unfortunately all subsequent nationalisms, starting with the German, were created as much out of resentment and fear of the most successful western European powers as out of any sense that European democracy was worth imitating. "Democracy" came to be interpreted as something quite different from representative government that was supposed to protect individuals from the abuse of power. Instead it came to be seen as the protection of the nation's interests at whatever costs. As long as all of the "people" were defended against outsiders, the nation's elite claimed that it was doing its duty. Therefore, nationalism increasingly came to justify autocratic militarization and violent exclusivity in the name of making the nation catch up to the more advanced West.

Also, the notion of nationalism in England, the United States, and in France was based on the idea that anyone who conformed to their cultures could be included as a citizen. In other societies that were less advanced, it was translated into something else: a sense that to be a member of the nation was like being a relative, connected by blood ties to other members of the nation. Thus whereas the original nationalism was civic, democratic, and based on behavior rather than on blood, later forms tended to be exclusive, autocratic, and based on assumed blood ties.

When nineteenth-century nationalists discovered Darwin's ideas about evolution of the fittest and the struggle for life, they drew the unfortunate conclusion that nations were species or races competing with each other

for space and resources. Nothing gave greater impetus to war and imperialism in the late nineteenth and early twentieth century than this
combination of Darwinian theories and nationalism.

The Legitimation of Commerce:
The Ideological Basis of the Industrial Revolution

Social theorists like Karl Marx, who are called *materialists*, believe that
ideas and moral precepts derive from material reality and interests. For
example, the rich invent religions that justify their wealth, whereas the
poor have to have such beliefs imposed on them by brute force and will
abandon them when given the chance and a proper education to show
them how they have been fooled. Materialists explain the great ideological changes that took place in Europe at the start of the modern era in the
same way. The market, that is the commercialization of land and labor,
and the greater ability to draw profits out of investments because of
technological innovation produced capitalism. Capitalism, in which markets determine who gets what and class predominates over prestige in
producing political power, is economically more efficient than the forms
of production that prevailed in agrarian societies, so the early capitalist
transformations in England and a few other European societies made
them the strongest in the world. They used this strength to impose their
will on the rest of the world and to create new, self-serving ideologies in
their own societies to justify the new power of money and markets.

There is obviously much truth to this, but the fact is that once a set of
beliefs or ideological view of the world exists, it has its own strength and
continues to influence perception even if the original conditions that
created such an idea have vanished. For example, religions created by
agrarian societies continue to have followers even in the most advanced
industrial societies, and there is no sign at all that Christianity, Islam,
Buddhism, or Hinduism are about to vanish. The ideas behind them are
convincing and powerful on their own.

Similarly, the ideological changes that accompanied the great transformation of agrarian society into industrial modernity are much more
complicated than a purely materialist explanation would suggest. There
was, to begin, the much older push toward rationalization of European
thought in the Renaissance and during the Protestant Reformation. This
occurred long before modern industrial society was on the horizon. This
is what Max Weber emphasized in his writings, and although it does not
contradict the materialist assumption that individuals and communities

think up ideologies that justify their own lives, it does make the argument more circuitous. In towns there was an incipient capitalist culture, but to explain why it became so powerful in Europe and not elsewhere requires more than simple awareness of the interests of merchants and manufacturers. If this new culture had remained simply that of urban merchants and had not led to a profound revolution in all aspects of thought, it would not have transformed the world.

Here we see the essence of cultural change and why it deviates from both biological change and the simplistic concepts of purely materialist thinkers. An idea may be so strong, so appealing, so illuminating, that it acquires a power of its own. Once it spreads, it will change societies, sometimes even overriding their material interests.

During the period of the Enlightenment in the eighteenth century, the systematic exploration of social and historical issues produced a startlingly new idea: that commerce and the pursuit of profit for its own sake was a morally valuable activity and could benefit society as a whole. No doubt, such a notion would not have gained much ground except in societies where commerce was of growing importance. But the idea that commercial activity was somehow morally good was so much at odds with the morality of all past agrarian societies that it reinforced and legitimized commercial pursuits in a way that had never been possible before. This strand of thinking, which was never fully accepted by all of Europe's thinkers, much less by all of its people, nevertheless proved convincing enough to provide a philosophical justification for expanding capitalism.

In older agrarian societies, except in a few merchant cities like Venice, some Muslim trading cities in Southeast Asia, and the ancient Phoenician ports, commerce was associated with greed and corruption. True honor went to fighting men, such as European knights or Japanese samurai, to otherworldly saints who escaped human turmoil, such as Hindu holy men or Buddhist monks, or to upright and loyal bureaucrats, such as the Confucian elite in China. For those who could not be part of the elite, the only honest occupation was agriculture, so that even if merchants were richer than poor peasants, they were considered a lower form of life. This almost instinctive reaction against commerce helped to preserve agrarian societies. It kept land from being sold and so maintained the solidarity of village communities. It prevented the more clever and enterprising commoners from getting ahead. It kept nobles and churchmen in power. In short, it kept the whole moral and political structure of agrarian societies intact. These societies recognized a very long time ago that giving free reign to entrepreneurship and the power of profit would be seriously disruptive because that rewarded innovation. We have already seen that in China just such an awareness during the Ming dynasty stopped long-distance trade and exploration, thus preventing the disruption of traditional ways that was about to begin in Europe.

The economist Albert Hirschman discovered in his research that throughout the Middle Ages in Europe it was thought that the pursuit of honor and community virtue was more noble than the pursuit of gain, which was seen as little more than greed. But eighteenth-century European thinkers, even before the full triumph of capitalism, began to see that the pursuit of honor led to endless war. Competition for honor is the pursuit of prestige for its own sake and for power over others simply to prove one's worth. Success for some means inevitable failure for others and kindles the desire for revenge. But commerce may be beneficial for everyone. Once some political philosophers recognized that improved economic performance may raise the general level of material well-being and that trading goods may be to the advantage of both buyer and seller, they suggested that more perfect societies could be created by honoring economic success over military honor, social prestige, or otherworldly withdrawal.

This led in the last part of the eighteenth century to the sophisticated theories of the Scottish economist Adam Smith. Smith understood that in general a free market in which people exchanged goods and services according to the rational calculation of their self-interest was likely to produce a more harmonious society than one in which exchanges were controlled for political or moral reasons.

As it was only subsequently that capitalism became the dominant form of economic organization, Hirschman concluded that a deep philosophical and ideological change occurred in the eighteenth century, and that without it, neither modernization nor capitalism would have advanced so quickly.

The novelty of a world view that actually placed economic activity and the search for profit in such an elevated place cannot be overemphasized. For most of the nineteenth and twentieth centuries, as this view proved itself to be correct and to explain the greater prosperity and freedom that market capitalist societies afforded their members, it was contested by discontented intellectuals trying to recreate mythical communal solidarities, angry traditionalists, and utopian promoters of egalitarianism. In essence, this has been the chief ideological drama of industrial societies.

The great discoveries of the Enlightenment eighteenth-century thinkers, far from being obsolete, remain original and prescient. They are still far from being widely accepted outside of a few advanced societies, but in the late twentieth century it is evident that these ideas are stronger than ever. By helping to legitimize capitalism in a few advanced societies, they prepared the way for the modern era, and they remain the essential philosophical guidelines to modernity.

Reference Notes
(Full references are in the bibliography)

The basic book on the rise of western Europe is Eric Jones's *The European Miracle*. He stresses Europe's ecological advantages. Douglass North and Robert Thomas wrote an earlier, much more theoretical explanation in *The Rise of the Western World*. Because North is one of the premier theoreticians of economic history in the world, this slim volume is well worth reading.

Max Weber, cited at the end of Chapter 2, developed the idea of religious rationalization as the basis of progress in the early modern era. Some of Robert Merton's essays in *Social Theory and Social Structure* amplify on this and on the connection between European religions and scientific progress.

Marc Bloch's *French Rural History* explains in great detail how a certain part of western Europe in the Middle Ages developed its agricultural technology, and how this formed the material basis of later progress.

Why China did not keep up with western Europe is explained by Mark Elvin's book cited at the end of Chapter 2. Frederic Wakeman's *The Fall of Imperial China* explains China's ancient pattern of dynastic cycles and how it was broken by contact with Europeans in the nineteenth century. Jonathan Spence's big but eminently readable *The Search for Modern China* also treats this subject and then goes on to provide the best available general history of China in the nineteenth and twentieth centuries.

Carlo Cipolla's *Guns, Sails and Empires* is the best brief account of how the West Europeans developed better ships and artillery than the rest of the world and how this allowed them to create the first global trading networks in the early modern era. Eric Wolf's *Europe and the People without History* traces the consequences of Europe's expansion on the rest of the world. He is particularly good in explaining the catastrophic demographic and social consequences of Europe's expansion on the natives of America.

For population figures, the McEvedy and Jones atlas cited at the end of Chapter 1 should be consulted.

The study of nationalism, which was in the doldrums for decades before the 1980s, has revived as everyone has realized that people's nationality has increasingly defined them in the modern age, and that nationalistic conflicts are getting worse, not slowly diminishing at the end of the twentieth century. The best works on this topic are by Ernest Gellner (*Nations and Nationalism*), Benedict Anderson (*Imagined Communities*), and the brilliantly original sociological history of the origins of European nationalism by Liah Greenfeld (*Nationalism*).

Albert Hirschman, the most imaginative contemporary economist to tackle the sociological and political aspects of economic theory, has explained the ideological origins of modern capitalism in his *The Passions and the Interests*. Another one of his books, *Exit, Voice, and Loyalty*, is the best short theoretical work on how markets really work.

4

The Modern Era

The quantitative changes in human societies produced by the advent of the modern industrial age are staggering. We have already seen that whereas the human population tripled roughly every fifteen thousand years in the preagrarian age, and about every fifteen hundred years in the agrarian era, the European population almost tripled in the nineteenth century (combining growth in Europe itself with the increase of the European population in the Americas through migration and natural increase). In the twentieth century the entire human population has more than tripled.

Other indicators of growth would show similarly astonishing changes. In 1800 well over 90 percent of the human population lived in rural villages or very small towns, and most of these people were peasants. On the whole, whether in Europe or elsewhere, they worked hard, were not free to move as they pleased or to dispose of their goods as they wished, paid high taxes to their lords, were illiterate, and had no foreseeable way of improving their lives. They had many children, but one third to one half, or in bad times even more, died before they reached the age of five.

By the late twentieth century in Europe, North America, Australia, Japan, and the other most advanced societies of East Asia, the vast majority of people live in cities or their adjacent suburbs. Almost all adults are literate. They have far fewer children, but almost all of them survive into adulthood. They pay an even higher portion of what they make in taxes than their peasant ancestors, but disposable income has gone up so much that the average inhabitant in these advanced societies has large amounts of money left over after paying for taxes and necessities. Much of the income of modern people is spent on what would have been considered unbelievable luxuries in the past: private cars, holiday trips, well-heated, clean, and spacious housing, durable and well-tailored clothing, immense varieties of healthy food available at low prices, and medical care that allows most people to live comfortably and productively into their sixties and seventies. It is a natural human propensity to complain and to claim that the present is worse than the past. But no one who has actually lived in an authentic, vermin-infested, socially and polit-ically oppressive agrarian village and compared this to life in a modern society can have many doubts about which one most people would prefer.

A proof of this is that the people from the remaining agrarian societies in the world have shown a very strong tendency to want to migrate to their own growing cities or to the advanced parts of the world. This is how the United States was populated by European immigrants fleeing from the poorer parts of western Europe, then later from central and eastern Europe, and then from East and Southeast Asia and from Latin America. This is how the cities of western Europe were filled by people from the hinterland escaping rural poverty, boredom, and social conser-vatism and repression, and why western Europe is now the target of migrations from the poorer parts of Europe, from Africa, and from Asia.

Within poorer countries themselves the old agrarian civilizations are breaking down, and societies in the late twentieth century have become far more urban, far richer, more mobile, and more literate. In the 1980s, about 80 percent of the population in advanced industrial societies lived in cities or suburbs. But even less advanced societies were becoming urbanized. By the 1980s more than half of the people in the Middle East and Latin America and close to a third of those in Africa were urban. Even in the last large reservoirs of peasant life in East, Southeast, and South Asia, in China, Indonesia, and India, almost one quarter of the population was urban by the 1980s. With the growth rate of cities in these places as high as it is, by the start of the twenty-first century their societies will be between one third and one half urban.

Without huge improvements in agricultural technology, of course, it would have been impossible for most people to cease being food produc-ers. Now in the most advanced countries 2 to 5 percent of the working population grow food, and they produce almost unmanageable surpluses.

Despite the widespread belief that world poverty is increasing, this is simply not true. Between 1950 and 1980 per capita production in Asia and Latin America roughly doubled. This is an economic growth rate some-what higher than that of the most advanced West European countries in the second half of the nineteenth century, and it matches the rates of economic growth experienced by the United States in the last decades of the nineteenth century and the early twentieth. To be sure, per capita economic production roughly tripled in the most advanced countries of the world in the period from 1950 to 1980, so that the gap in average well-being between rich and poor countries increased, but this is not the same as saying that the poor got poorer.

In fact, it is only in a few countries such as Ghana, Zaire, Ethiopia, Burma, Cambodia, or Haiti that the population actually became poorer during the second half of the twentieth century, and this can be attributed directly to gross political mismanagement, corruption, or civil war. In the 1990s large numbers of people in the former communist countries of Eastern Europe and the Soviet Union have also become poorer, but again, this is the result of decades of preceding political mismanagement, faulty policies, and the bloody wars that have accompanied the collapse of communism.

The modernization that began in western Europe has now spread throughout most of the world and irrevocably changed societies. This is because West European societies evolved a way of life that produces stronger and better adapted societies than those that existed before. This hardly means that other societies are on their way to being physically exterminated by the Europeans, but that their cultures and social systems are being irrevocably altered.

It would be possible to give production statistics that underlie the vast progress made during the modern era: steel production, tons of coal mined, square meters of cloth manufactured, numbers of automobiles that have come off assembly lines, and so on. As far as most of us are concerned, however, it is not such production figures that matter but how our lives and the perception of our lives have changed.

Emphasizing the purely material aspects of change in the modern era can be misleading. If most people are better off than their ancestors, this does not mean that there are no problems associated with modernization. On the contrary, the rapidity of change has had a wrenching effect on all the societies affected. Even in the most advanced parts of Europe these changes have occurred only in the past six to eight generations, and throughout most of the world, only in the past two to four generations. Thus human societies have not yet had time to absorb the consequences of all these transformations or to find workable solutions to all the problems they have produced. After all, it took two thousand years for agrarian-state societies to work out religious and ideological solutions to the moral problems raised by the changes they brought about. It will take at least a few centuries for modern industrial social systems to do the same.

Furthermore, the intellectual, religious, and political elites who produce the ideas through which human societies interpret their world have been far from universally happy about modernization. Many have devoted their lives over the past two hundred years to resisting modernization, denigrating it, and proposing ways of reorganizing societies to nullify the effects of capitalism, markets, and industrialization. If material progress throughout the modern era had always been smooth, without periodic crises, and if it had been evenly distributed, so that all parts of every society had gained at an equal rate, these intellectuals would have had few listeners. But social change in the modern era has been anything but smooth and evenly distributed.

It is to the problems raised by modernization that we must now turn in order to better understand social and cultural change in the past two centuries.

Industrial Cycles

The Industrial Revolution is usually thought to have begun in England in about 1780. Though no economic change can be dated precisely, it is certain that between 1760 and 1800 a major change took place. Wool and linen cloth manufacturing were vastly surpassed by the production of manufactured cotton cloth, and this cotton cloth started to be made in factories that were more mechanized than any large-scale manufacturing process had ever been before. In the 1750s to 1770s, England, which can grow no cotton because it is too cold, imported an average of one to three thousand metric tons of cotton per year, mostly from India. By 1790 that shot up to 14,000 tons per year, by 1800 to 24,000, by 1810 to 56,000, and by 1840 to 208,000 tons. By that time, the South in the United States had become the world's major producer of cotton. The spectacular inventiveness of entrepreneurs in England yielded a long set of mechanical improvements that allowed cloth to be made faster, better, and more cheaply than ever before in human history, so that English cloth exports gained markets all over the world. Other advanced European countries and eventually the United States imitated England's technology, but it took decades to catch up, and during this time the English combined their advantage in cloth making with their older skills in shipping and long-distance trade to become by far the dominant economic power in the world. None of this would have been possible if private entrepreneurship had not been considered legitimate or if profits had been restricted for social reasons.

Yet even in England the social changes produced by this transformation were resisted. The increasing marketization of land and agricultural products forced out inefficient producers and broke up village communities. The English tried to pass welfare laws that would subsidize those who stayed in their native villages and small towns. But the pressures of the market were too strong, and those who considered capitalism legitimate were now too powerfully entrenched. Allowing labor mobility was as important a part of the growth of the English economy as allowing owners of capital to invest and sell as they wished, and restrictive laws that tried to keep poor villagers at home were removed to allow free entry into the factory labor force.

The first phase of the industrial era, that based on improvements in textile manufacturing, lasted from about the 1780s until the 1830s and 1840s. But already by the 1820s it had produced the first of the great, periodic crises that have marked the industrial era. Excess investment in textile production, increasing competition, both in England and in other European countries, and relative saturation of the market meant that the less efficient producers were driven into bankruptcy.

In the early days of the textile cycle of the industrial age, less modern, less mechanized producers had been able to benefit from the general boom. Now those small artisans and producers who could not keep up with the costs of further mechanical improvements were ruined, thus throwing many workers and independent small owners of looms out of work.

It was the observation of the social crisis that this produced in the 1820s and 1830s in England and, about a decade later, through the 1840s in other textile centers of western Europe, that led Karl Marx to develop his theories about how capitalism would fail. With time new technological improvements would yield ever less of a return as they were copied, and to keep up with the competition, manufacturers would be obliged to cut wages. The workers would become impoverished. But meanwhile the fantastic efficiency of capitalist competition would also ruin old-fashioned independent artisans and producers too weak to keep up with the rising cost of new machinery. So, in the end, a few very efficient manufacturers would take over the entire economy while the rest of the population would be forced to become very poor, virtually enslaved workers.

This was a dark vision that promised that industrial society would be even poorer and less free than agrarian societies, where at least peasants were somewhat protected by their village communities and customs. But redemption could come through revolution. Eventually the workers would organize to overthrow the system, and there would be socialism. Thus the beneficial technological ingenuity of modern capitalism would be harnessed by socially aware forces; the irrationalities of overproduction and the inequities of early capitalism would be eradicated. Furthermore, the modern sense of alienation, of separation from community and morality imposed by the ruthlessness of market forces, would be overcome in socialism. The supposed warmth of the original, preindustrial family and village would be recreated.

It was a view of history that was quite similar to the Christian vision. In the beginning, said Marx, there was perfect equality and a strong sense of community—a kind of Garden of Eden. Then, with the coming of agrarian societies, there was the invention of private property, of social stratification, and of inequality and oppression. The few with power and property used these to enrich themselves while the masses were enslaved. Capitalism was making the situation even worse and destroying what was left of community and social solidarity by intensifying competition and greed. But then a prophet, Karl Marx, would come to show the way to a better future. Eventually there would be a great battle between the forces of good and evil, a kind of apocalyptic Armageddon. The struggle would be won by the forces of good, that is the Marxist socialists, and humanity would be saved; it would return to a paradise in which all property would be communal, there would be perfect equality, and general happiness would reign.

No nineteenth-century social thinker proposed as seductive a vision as Karl Marx, and none was as influential in the twentieth. Marxists always claimed to be hostile to religion. Indeed they were, but that was because they offered their own substitute faith. They claimed that they had scientific proof, based on the study of economic history, that their vision would prove correct. But in reality this was the first of the great new religions thrown up by the Industrial Revolution, based on as much wishful thinking as the faiths it was supposed to replace. We will see what it led to.

Marx's vision was based on a complete misunderstanding of industrial cycles. The progress of capitalism did not cease with the growing troubles of the textile-led economy. A new "high-tech" product was invented, the railroad, that became, literally as well as figuratively, the engine of an enormous new burst of growth. The railroad, unlike the mechanical loom, was an invention that was out in the open for everyone to see, and it was a marvel of modern engineering. It made cheap and rapid land transportation available for the first time in human history. It brought remote regions into contact with the rest of the world. It greatly lowered the cost of transporting people and bulk goods. Thus it revolutionized all aspects of the economy and brought modernization everywhere it went.

Along with railroads there had to be a variety of other industrial products. Demand for iron and coal went up. Steam engines were perfected, and this had an effect on all spheres of production.

In the second cycle of the industrial era, which lasted from the 1840s to the 1870s, the railroad and iron cycle, England continued to dominate the world. It was able to use its accumulated capital and expertise in engineering, commerce, and manufacturing in the new industries. The wave of social unrest that had troubled much of western Europe from the 1820s to the 1840s died down as new jobs were created, new industries flourished, and general prosperity returned.

Then in the early 1870s another collapse occurred. By now transportation and communications were much better, and the European economies were more closely tied with each other and with that of the United States, so that a nearly simultaneous depression rolled over the entire advanced world. There had been too much railroad construction, and many companies went bankrupt. The boom had created too much supply of many goods, and a string of bankruptcies ensued. Stock markets crashed in 1873, and once again it began to seem that Marx's predictions were right. Capitalism was in crisis and might soon come to an end as labor militancy rose and the threat of socialist revolution began to frighten the authorities.

But the passing of the second industrial cycle in the 1870s only heralded the start of a third phase. This time, the leading "high-tech" products were organic chemicals (used at first to produce dyes for textiles), steel (which replaced iron), and, in the 1880s, electrical machinery.

Just as railroads had seemed a fantastic product of high technology, so did the new discoveries bring about more wonders. This time, however, there was something new. Textile manufacturing had used not advanced science but inspired tinkering and clever entrepreneurship to make its advances. Railroads were much closer to being a product of genuine scientific progress, but even there, the actual scientific knowledge required to make such machines, if not yet the engineering, had been available for many decades. But with the advent of organic chemistry as a vital component of industry, pure scientific research came into its own. It required advanced scientists to keep up with what was going on, and the first society to actively finance research into this area through its universities, Germany, gained a huge advantage. From the last part of the nineteenth century on, the relationship between science and technology became much more direct, and only those societies willing and able to finance scientific research could hope to keep up. This meant that scientific research now received much more financing than ever before from both governments and private firms eager to find new processes and products.

The third industrial cycle also saw something else. Contrary to the expectations of Karl Marx and other foes of capitalism, the most advanced industries no longer needed just masses of poorly paid unskilled laborers. Growing technological sophistication required a better educated work force.

It is not surprising, therefore, that the two Western societies that invested the most in the late nineteenth century in research universities and in giving a larger proportion of their population a sound secondary education, the United States and Germany, moved ahead of England. England did not lose ground in any absolute sense, but it grew more slowly and lost its primary position in the world economy.

But the intense international competition produced by Germany's rise as the major European economy increased tensions. This was combined with an interpretation of Darwin's work (first published in 1859) that made intellectuals and leaders believe that nations were locked in the same kinds of competition for survival as biological organisms. The belief that to be fit and survive it was necessary to expand produced not only a mad race for colonies outside of Europe but an armaments race, and eventually the First World War.

This war, which went from 1914 to 1918, marked the end of the third industrial cycle, and again produced widespread belief that capitalism and its attendant political innovations, democracy and greater respect for individual freedom, were now obsolete. Yet once again, despite the difficulty of adjusting to a new industrial cycle, capitalism did not end. In the 1920s and 1930s there began the fourth period, the age of automobiles, petrochemicals, and mass-produced mechanical consumer goods. This started in the United States and was marked by an enormous increase in the availability of high-technology popular goods such as refrigerators, cars, and radios. World War II, fought from 1939 to 1945, interrupted this cycle, but it resumed again in the 1950s and spread its benefits to large parts of the world. Rapid advances in airplane technology made very rapid transportation throughout the world possible. In this period the world economy was dominated by the United States.

By about 1970, however, new signs of trouble began to appear. Competitors in Japan and western Europe were gaining ground on the United States. Throughout the formerly most advanced industrial parts of the world, obsolete plants with highly paid workers were starting to lose money. New factories and entire new industries sprang up, making the industrial giants of the previous industrial cycles vulnerable. Just as the textile manufacturing heartland of England had suffered at the time of the end of the first industrial cycle, so now the Middle West in the United States, the industrial cities of Great Britain, of northern France, of Belgium, and in the Ruhr Valley of Germany faced declining employment, intense pressure to lower high wages, and a string of bankruptcies of venerable old firms. Within the United States new industrial regions in the West and South prospered while old centers declined. In Germany it was Bavaria that made gains against the older industrial centers. But because of the crisis in the old centers of industrial production there was again a sense that capitalism was on the verge of failure. As always at the end of one industrial cycle and the start of another, uncertainty produced growing social unrest in the 1960s and 1970s. This period also saw the high point of Marxism.

Marxist revolutionaries had taken power in Russia in 1917, in Eastern Europe after 1945, in China in 1949, in North Vietnam in 1954, in Cuba in 1959, and in South Vietnam, Laos, and Cambodia after a long war against the United States in 1975. It began to seem that Marxist socialism was the inevitable future of the world and that capitalism was doomed to decline in crisis and internal unrest. But this was no more the case in the 1970s than it had been in the 1920s and 1930s, in the 1870s and 1880s, or in the 1830s and 1840s.

Instead the 1970s saw the start of the fifth industrial cycle. This one, in which we still live, has been dominated by electronics, and as it progresses the highest of "high-tech" products will be biomedical. The basis of these changes was, first of all the transistor and then the silicon computer chip. As in past industrial cycles, innovations in one area spread quickly to others. Automobile, machine tool, and textile manufacturing were all revolutionized by the new technologies. Computers have made communications fantastically faster than ever before and have made it possible to store and manipulate giant amounts of information. This in turn has changed business practices as well as accelerated scientific research.

But the most momentous changes of the fifth industrial cycle are still to happen. Advances in fundamental theoretical biology in the 1950s, the discovery of how genes work, has led in the 1980s and 1990s to the start of a whole new branch of the economy. Biomedical manufacturing is just beginning, but it will revolutionize agriculture as well as other aspects of economic life. It will also begin to produce miracle medical products as dramatic as those that came in the first half of the twentieth century when a variety of infectious diseases were brought under control. Whereas the world demand for certain goods such as food, textiles, televisions, or cars

may soon reach an upper limit, the demand for greater health and lon-
gevity is unlikely to be sated at any time soon. Those who believed in the
past that capitalism was doomed because of overproduction and sated
demand will be proved as wrong this time as in the past. Each new industrial cycle brings enormous new demand in previously unanticipated
sectors, as well as new jobs, new opportunities for profit, and a thorough
renewal as old, seemingly all-powerful firms lose ground to more innovative little enterprises.

In the late nineteenth century it was feared in the United States that a
few railroad magnates would take control of the country. In the early
1900s those who feared the power of the biggest capitalist firms thought
that Carnegie (U.S. Steel) and Rockefeller (Standard Oil) would take over
the world. In the 1950s it was thought that General Motors might become
so powerful that it would come to dominate the globe. In the 1970s IBM
seemed poised to take on this role. In the 1990s, a giant firm that did not
even exist in the 1970s, Microsoft, is considered dangerously powerful by
its enemies. No doubt in the first decade of the next century some as yet
unknown biotech firm will appear out of nowhere and threaten to mo-
nopolize the economy. Of course, no one knows if it will be a European,
a Japanese, or an American firm. But the pattern repeats itself, and will
continue to do so for a long time to come.

The only certainty is that education and scientific research will continue to play an ever increasing role in determining economic success.
And those societies that apply this lesson best will dominate the future
even more surely than England did in most of the nineteenth century and
the United States in most of the twentieth.

Internal and International Social Consequences of Modernization and Industrial Cycles

The social consequences of the Industrial Revolution were enormous.
Some have already been mentioned: urbanization, very rapid population
growth, a much higher level of education for the average person, the
transformation of old solidarities in favor of a more individualistic,
market-driven type of behavior, and great improvements in material
well-being. There were many others. Families became smaller. They had
fewer children, and because of much greater physical mobility, fewer
close relatives continued living near each other. Monetary calculations
became a much more important part of daily life because virtually all eco-

nomic life was monetized; that is, whereas in the past peasants directly raised much of their own food and made many of the goods they needed, modern workers are paid in money and buy what they need. Almost no family still produces a significant proportion of the necessities it needs to live.

At one time or another all of these changes have been resisted, either by the leaders of the agrarian societies being transformed, who were afraid of losing status and power, or by idealistic intellectuals who wanted to regain a purer, less materialistic way of life, or by people thrown out of work and home by the attendant economic changes. It was said that working for money instead of directly producing goods is unwholesome and alienating. Smaller families were called lonely. Spending too much time in school was said to deprive children of a healthy existence. Obliging everyone to calculate their actions in terms of how much money they stood to make or lose was said to be dishonorable and unnatural. Turning life into a series of rational economic calculations, which is what sound market behavior consists of, was deemed boring, and many intellectuals said that it robbed the modern world of beauty and poetry, as did the machines produced by the Industrial Revolution.

These types of criticism were common enough among intellectuals and also among old elites who were losing ground in the best of times. But they became particularly acute and elicited widespread sympathy during those moments of crisis when industrial cycles were in their declining periods. Such declines have brought about a series of recurring problems that intensified the sense of alienation and unfairness created by the uneven spread of modernization.

By going through the three main sets of problems produced by the declining phase of industrial cycles we can see why there is a certain repetitive pattern to the kinds of complaints raised against each of them. As industrial cycles continue to occur, we can predict that the same kinds of problems will recur in the future, and so will the complaints and hostile reactions to continuing modernization.

The first set of problems that beset societies in the declining phase of an industrial cycle is a function of the loss of competitiveness of certain firms and geographic areas because of changes in technology. What were highly successful firms and areas may find themselves bypassed, and previously well-paid laborers may be forced to take cuts in pay or even become unemployed. To some extent, migration can take care of this problem, and firms or areas with sufficiently balanced infrastructures can adapt and survive. But readjustment always entails some suffering, and of course those caught by such problems are upset and seek explanations. They also seek redress, by political means if that seems possible. This is why Marx was certain that eventually, during a moment of crisis, the workers would organize a revolution that would end capitalism once and for all.

But of course the first industrial age gave way to the second, and that in turn to the third, fourth, and fifth. Each time new technologies were invented that took pressure off the economy by providing new sources of profit, new employment, and a higher level of productivity. Cyclical crises in the past have always ended with capitalist economies at higher standards of living, with higher real wages, and with new periods of accommodation between capital and labor. In the long run economic change has been anything but a zero-sum game, with any winner having to be balanced by a loser, though in the short run, during periods of crisis, it has been a different story.

There has been a second, parallel set of problems associated with major industrial shifts. The first industrial age was dominated by England, the most advanced and powerful economy of its day. The accumulated capital and experience gained by England during this age allowed it to dominate the second, railway and iron age too. But the third age was different. Germany, and even before its unification in 1871, the individual German states, tended to support university scientific research much better than the English, and they reaped rewards for this. Also, Germany, like the United States, educated a considerably larger portion of its population than the English (or for that matter the French).

So Germany and the United States moved ahead of England in this age, and it was particularly the German success that was striking because Germany did not have the immense advantage of endless resources and cheap immigrant labor possessed by the United States. Also, Germany threatened England's hegemony in Europe much more directly. This problem eventually led to the mad race for empires that dominated international relations in the last part of the nineteenth century and finally produced World War I.

But the feeling shared by the great and medium powers of the world during that time was based on a thorough misunderstanding of how progress and economic success worked. Just as Marx felt that technological progress in industrial societies had to be a zero-sum game in the end, with the workers losing whatever capital they might gain, so did the statesmen and generals and captains of industry in the late nineteenth century believe that progress and prosperity had to be zero-sum games.

Countries that could not protect their markets and sources of raw materials by acquiring colonies had to suffer for it. It was barely understood, if at all, that education and research were the basis of Germany's strength, not its army and martial bearing.

Though it took a long time to produce the conditions that led to World War I, it can be shown that the fundamental problem was failure by the Europeans to adjust to the third industrial cycle or to understand its implications.

Similarly, the aftermath of Word War I was bad enough, but the coincident shift from the third to the fourth industrial period compounded the problem. In the fourth industrial age, research and education assumed an ever greater importance, but so did something quite new. Automobiles and the spread of electrical consumer appliances demanded a rapidly broadening mass consumer base. The Great Depression of the 1930s was primarily a failure of demand to keep up with increasing productivity. What would have been required was a highly stimulating macroeconomic policy on the part of the main industrial powers, chiefly the United States, the only country able to go through the transformation of the fourth industrial age in the 1920s. But the United States did not follow such a policy, particularly abroad, and this made it virtually impossible for the world economy to adjust to the changes occurring.

In contrast to this, the United States after World War II refloated the world economy and created the conditions for the greatest economic boom in history. During that time, the fourth industrial age flourished; its benefits spread throughout the advanced Western countries and Japan and even began to spread beyond that into formerly poor countries. But now that age has ended, and the United States is losing the hegemonic preponderance it once had. The transition to the fifth industrial age, though unlikely to be as rocky as some of the past transitions, will not be without its problems. That is what much of the discussion about the decline of the United States in the 1980s and 1990s has been about.

There is no question that the transition from one cycle to another produces great international stress. Nationalism, an invention of the modern era, intensifies. Competition seems to take on a particularly bitter edge because of the fear that a temporary downturn is really the beginning of a final collapse. And those who are gaining at the expense of others demand greater power and privilege in the world political system, while the old hegemons try to keep their power intact. The possibility of conflict between major advanced countries is therefore greatest during the shift from one industrial age to another.

The third problem associated with the industrial era is the problem of backwardness. Of course, there were always more or less advanced parts of the world, but only in the modern era has backwardness become so perilous. Only since the industrialized revolution have the technological advantages of the leading industrial nations given them the potential to dominate the more backward regions so thoroughly. Ever since this perception has come into being, ideological solutions have been proposed.

One, first suggested by the German economist Friedrich List in the mid-nineteenth century, has been at the heart of a whole number of nationalist economic theories that have tried to overcome backwardness, among both socialist governments and supposedly very conservative ones. That is to close off developing economies from world markets in order to give them a chance to establish their own industrial base. The idea is that the advanced economies are just too efficient to take on. But this solution has produced very uneven results, generally making the protected economies weak and uncompetitive. Today the search for a solution continues, and as we saw earlier, the gap between the richest and poorest countries continues to grow.

The perception of international unfairness is an important cause of anticapitalist and anti-Western ideological movements in the more backward parts of the world. It is clear that Western science and technology are superior and that they must be adopted to some extent. But the feeling that the established industrial powers are simply using their economic and political muscle to keep other societies poor exacerbates jealousy and resentful nationalism. It creates a climate of deep resentment among the proud intellectuals of backward countries, and this in turn makes them treat with contempt the ideologies of individualism and democracy practiced by the most successful Western countries. They claim that even though they are technologically more backward, at least they have maintained traditional communal solidarities and less materialistic values. They claim to be morally superior to the greedy and exploitative West.

Thus the social tensions of modernization, exacerbated by the industrial cycles that have caused disruptions even in the most advanced economies, have led to a variety of political protest movements within advanced societies and internationally.

Class, Status, and Power in Modern Societies

Just as the invention of agriculture and the state drastically changed the pattern of social stratification, the distribution of power and privilege in human societies, so did the Industrial Revolution. Peasants gradually disappeared. This most numerous of classes, which included the vast majority of human beings who lived between the third millennium B.C. and the twentieth century A.D., virtually vanished in less than 150 years in the advanced societies of the world. The old nobilities who had controlled the land and been a military elite in most agrarian societies vanished at about the same time. Almost all of the princes, kings, and emperors who had ruled agrarian societies lost their powers or were eliminated entirely. Though cities grew enormously the old urban merchant and artisan classes were transformed beyond recognition.

The new economic classes that replaced the old ones were, at the top, owners and controllers of capital: entrepreneurs, financiers, and top managers of businesses. Immediately below them there developed a class of specialized professionals—doctors, lawyers, engineers, researchers and educators, journalists—whose advanced education and skills were necessary to keep ever more complex economies and societies functioning smoothly. Below them there grew a large new class of people who were neither owners of businesses nor highly qualified specialists, but bureaucratic, low-level managers. These kinds of white-collar occupations also proliferated in government machines that became increasingly bureaucratic and intrusive as modernization advanced and the powers of the state to administer society grew. Yet one more level below them were another growing class, clerical workers, who formed a kind of lower middle class with higher aspirations. Finally, those who provided most of the labor during the first century and a half of the Industrial Revolution were the growing working class. There remained those in agriculture, but these now metamorphosed from peasants into farmers: business managers and entrepreneurs on the land following the dictates of the market rather than of tradition or community restrictions.

The multiplication of special professions and the continual changes in technology over the life of the five industrial cycles have continued to change class structures in modern societies.

In England in about 1870 about 4 to 5 percent of all households were in what could be considered the "middle class," that is, what used to be called the "bourgeoisie" (which comes from the French term for townsmen). These were the owners and managers of enterprises and the new professionals. Above them there still remained the old aristocracy, and below them were the clerks in the lower middle class and the workers who were in the new urban lower class. Only a very small number of the new bourgeoisie was rich or owned much property. Most owners of enterprises had small businesses rather than very large ones, and most of the new bourgeoisie worked for others instead of for their own businesses. But even so, this class was of growing importance. By the early twentieth century the bourgeoisie included close to 10 percent of the households in England and slightly more than that in the United States. If the lower middle class, the clerical workers who aspired to being bourgeois, is included, the middle class as a whole included about 20 percent of the households in the most advanced Western societies of the early twentieth century.

Nothing quite like it had ever existed before. The number of people between the princes and nobles on one hand and the peasants on the other had always been quite small in agrarian societies. Now they were not only many of them, but they were educated and politically aware, and they demanded privileges and rights that underlings had never had before. They also found important and powerful allies in the upper bourgeoisie, the most successful entrepreneurs, financiers, owners, and managers who controlled the productive resources of modern societies. All were interested in reducing the powers of the old aristocracies, in promoting government action to keep markets free, and in allowing political representation of the middle class. They shared a common ideology of nationalism and distrust of the lower classes.

Not only did the bourgeoisie as a whole become politically more powerful as it took over the main roles in the economy, but the way in which its members lived set the standards for society as a whole. They were utilitarian, business oriented, and practical. They believed in hard work, thrift, and sexual self-control. Their families were the primary focus of their social lives and economic calculations. Their cultural tastes and habits have been named after the Queen of England who reigned from 1837 to 1901, "Victorian."

"Victorian bourgeois" values have been derided by intellectuals and by opponents of capitalism, especially its British and American forms, from the late nineteenth century until the present. Yet these repressed, disciplined, striving people were actually carrying forward the old values of the rational townspeople who had begun the transformation of the European economy and made modernization possible. Bourgeois culture was highly adaptive and successful in modern societies. Not only did it make individual families successful, but the spread of these habits throughout other social classes, particularly into the working class, created the self-restraint, discipline, and order necessary to make industrial systems work.

It turns out that in the late twentieth century the most dynamic societies in the world, those of East Asia, are dominated by a growing middle class whose hard work, thrift, desire for education, ambitions for their children, and self-control closely approximate the Victorian bourgeois culture of western Europe and the United States in the late nineteenth and early twentieth century.

By the late twentieth century, in the most advanced societies, the middle class makes up close to 30 percent of the population, and the lower middle class, another 25 percent. These two classes now make up the majority of the population of advanced societies, though in the West their values and habits have become much more lax than when they were still "Victorian."

Karl Marx foresaw the day when the working class, those who worked in factories, transportation, or mining to actually make products or operate machines, would eventually make up most of the population in modern societies. As peasants left the land and industry grew, this did seem to be the trend. In the United States, for example, this class made up 48 percent of the households in 1910, a huge increase over the situation in the early nineteenth century when industry was just starting to develop. But then growth slowed, with only 52 percent of the households in 1950 being working class. And with the advent of the fifth industrial age, the demand for such jobs declined. By 1982, only 44 percent of households in the United States were working class, and by 2000 only about one third will be. This means that the growth of professional and white-collar jobs has increased so fast that this portion of the working population has actually become larger than the industrial working class. The political power of the workers, which rose as they unionized to demand higher wages and more political representation, peaked in the 1950s and 1960s in the advanced industrial economies. Since then it has been declining.

The distribution of the population by class does not, however, explain stratification patterns fully. As in agrarian societies, certain groups may have high prestige, or status, without controlling the economy. This was the case with the descendants of the European aristocracies throughout the nineteenth century and through the first half of the twentieth. As they lost their political monopoly, and as blood or titles ceased to be tickets to automatic wealth, they lost their distinctive class role. But their prestige was so high that the richest members of the upper bourgeoisie tried to imitate their ways. In certain branches of the government, particularly as military officers, the old nobilities remained important, and their codes of honor and behavior became those of the new, enlarged European armies. Even in the United States, which had no hereditary nobility, a kind of pseudoaristocracy with fake traditions was invented. The most prestigious secondary schools and universities, social clubs, and military officers took on the ways of European aristocrats and pretended to be more concerned with blood and upbringing than with crass money.

To some extent this preoccupation with prestige explains the great concern European states in the late nineteenth century had with honor and military prestige. This contributed to the conditions that led to imperialism and aggressive wars. Aristocratic prestige also played a role as a rallying force against the forces of modernization and democracy throughout the first half of the twentieth century. To this day cultural remnants of aristocratic attitudes remain widespread among intellectuals who disdain business, practicality, and the boredom of bourgeois morality.

Neither class nor status structure is sufficient to account for the distribution of power in modern societies. To be sure, the rising middle class took a larger share of power in the nineteenth and twentieth centuries, and the richest owners of businesses gained a disproportionate share of that power. Older and fading elites used their high status to hold on to some power well into the twentieth century in Europe, and they continue to be important in many poorer countries. But modern societies also have professional politicians and government officials who pursue power for its own sake, not to defend any particular class or interest group.

Officials or soldiers whose main base of power is their control over the state are not a modern invention. The Confucian bureaucrats in China were powerful in their own right, and though they used their official posts to acquire wealth and land, ultimately their administrative rank determined their influence and ability to enrich themselves. Similarly, mercenary soldiers in the Middle East from the tenth century until the nineteenth frequently exercised political power. Sheer force—the ability to impose their will through violence—and not control of property or high prestige was the base of their power.

In modern states it is more difficult for mercenary armies to take power, though military officers have seized control on many occasions. But bureaucrats have become more powerful than they ever were, even in China. The modern state controls a much larger proportion of society's gross product than states could ever use in the past. In the United States, for example, all governments (local, state, and federal) spent about 8 percent of the total gross national product (all goods and services produced by the economy) in 1913. By the 1940, that proportion had gone up to 20 percent. By the 1970s and 1980s, that proportion had gone up to 35 percent. The United States, it should be said, has a somewhat lower percentage of its gross national product controlled by government than the advanced countries of western Europe. In most of them, governments control close to 50 percent of the gross national product.

Government officials have become a class in and of themselves. Though they do not own their means of production, they have a vested interest in keeping their jobs and expanding their privileges. The only check on their tendency to expand their power and privilege is the existence of elected officials who set their budgets and are supposed to be responsive to the will of the general population. In dictatorships where such officials do not exist—for example, in the communist states that disintegrated in the late 1980s and early 1990s—top bureaucrats became the ruling class. Like the Confucian officials in classical China, they stifled innovation, took too much power, and caused their societies to stagnate.

In capitalist societies, where private ownership of the means of production and elected officials keep control over the bureaucracy, the situation is much better. Yet elected officials themselves can easily become a distinct class, using their power to accumulate personal wealth and putting aside the interests of their constituents in order to preserve their own. If they work too closely with the bureaucrats they are meant to oversee, it can be difficult to get society's larger interests represented.

One of the worst mistakes made by Marxist social theorists was their failure to recognize that in all societies, even in capitalist ones, control of the economic means of production is hardly the only route to political power. Prestige may help, too. But professional politicians and bureaucrats become a virtual class able to override the interests of others in order to preserve themselves.

Roberto Michels, an early twentieth-century German-Italian sociologist, formulated what he called the "Iron Law of Oligarchy." This was based on his observation of the growing socialist parties in Europe at that time. Supposedly created to defend the interests of the working class, and closely tied to unions, they quickly came to be ruled by professional politicians and administrators whose first goal was to strengthen their own positions and only then to look out for the interests of their supposed constituents. This tendency is almost universal in even the most democratic political systems. Parties are created to further certain interests and ideologies, but they become machines whose primary function is to keep themselves in power in order to enjoy its fruits.

There is little question that the only way to keep any control over the power of the modern state, of political parties, or of state bureaucracies is to have periodic elections and changes in power. When that becomes impossible, as in dictatorships, increasing corruption and repression of dissent become almost inevitable.

The main political difference between the most successful modern societies of the twentieth century and agrarian societies is that a mechanism for the renewal of power through the periodic displacement of elites is available. That is the chief function of democracy: not to represent all the various interests in a modern society perfectly, which is impossible, but to limit the tenure and power of the professional power seekers and to keep some control over corruption.

Despite all the potential for concentration of power in ever more powerful governments, modern societies cannot maintain the highly unequal structure of reward that characterized agrarian societies. An industrial economy needs too many educated people who demand a greater share of the rewards available. High education and concentration of people in urban areas makes political organization easier, and interest groups resist the imposition of policies that hurt them. In this respect, Marx was correct. Not only the middle classes, but the working class and other groups have been able to organize far more successfully than nonelites ever could in agrarian societies, and this has placed a limit on how great a share of the surplus wealth small elites can take.

Data from the World Bank indicate that in the 1980s income distribution in the richest, most modernized countries was more equitable than in the poorest countries. But in the middle-ranked countries, it was most inequitable of all. This may reflect a historical pattern, in which income becomes more highly concentrated as industrialization occurs, but then becomes better distributed as interest groups become better organized and the society becomes wealthier as a whole (see Table 4-1).

If only the three middle categories are considered, in the richest industrialized countries those middle 60 percent of the population received 54 percent of the national income. In the middle-income countries, those 60 percent received only 39 percent of the national income, and in the poor countries they received 43 percent of the national income. The poorest 20 percent of the population in rich countries receive a higher share of the national income than in poor or middling countries. But the biggest difference is for the rich, who receive only 40 percent of the national income in rich countries but well over 50 percent in poorer countries.

The same World Bank data confirm this by showing that the top 10 percent of the population received, on average, 37 percent of the income in the poor countries, 44 percent of the income in the middle-income countries, and only 24 percent of the income in the richest countries.

TABLE 4-1

Income Distribution by Fifths of the Population

	Percentage of the National Income Received by Each Fifth				
Type of Country	*Poorest 5th*	*4th 5th*	*3rd 5th*	*2nd 5th*	*Top 5th*
Poorest[a]	6	8	13	22	52
Middle Income[b]	4	8	12	19	58
Richest[c]	7	12	18	24	40

Source: Based on The World Bank, *World Development Report 1989.*
a. Data for India, Kenya, and Indonesia averaged.
b. Data for Egypt, Mexico, and Brazil averaged.
c. Data for France, Germany, Japan, and the U.S. averaged.

Though it is not certain that a comparison of poor and rich countries in the 1980s reproduces the historical trend in advanced societies in the past, an examination of data from the United States and England in the twentieth century suggests that in these cases the pattern was the same. These two advanced societies became much more egalitarian in the twentieth century, particularly in the 1930s to 1960s, than they had been in the late nineteenth and early twentieth centuries. The great concentrations of wealth produced by the first several cycles of the industrial revolution raised the general welfare but also concentrated wealth. During the fourth industrial cycle, however, there was a trend toward greater equality. This was particularly necessary because this cycle was based on the distribution of expensive consumer goods. In the fifth industrial cycle, we may be experiencing a partial drift back toward greater inequality as those with adequate education continue to make gains while the less skilled find fewer job opportunities.

The examination of class, status, and power in modern societies has left us with a set of paradoxes. The potential for centralized bureaucratic rule obviously increased with modernization; yet in the most successful capitalist societies there has been a trend toward democratization of politics and greater income equality. The spread of commerce and manufacturing has made it possible to overcome many of the problems of agrarian societies; however, we know that the recurring problems caused by periodic industrial cycles continue to create conflict within and between different societies. No period in human history has so liberated individuals, but even a cursory look at the political history of the twentieth century will show that it has experienced the most brutal wars and forms of ruthless dictatorship ever witnessed in history.

To begin to address these contradictions it is necessary to review the ideologies and forms of political protest that have characterized the modern world.

Political Ideologies and Protests: Two Centuries of Revolutions

For an economic historian, the modern, industrial era began some time in the last third or quarter of the eighteenth century. For a historian of ideas it started a bit earlier, with the English and French Enlightenment political philosophers who wrote in the late seventeenth and eighteenth centuries. For a political historian who can date changes more precisely by dramatic events, the modern political era began either with the American Revolution of 1775 or the French Revolution of 1789.

It is easy to confuse the general sweep of history with the particular causes of this or that event. Many European intellectuals in the late eighteenth century understood that the old political systems of agrarian states would not be able to survive unchanged in an age when philosophers were proclaiming that proper government had to be a compact between the people and their state in which individuals were protected from arbitrary power. Nor were they unaware that the social changes that accompanied rising commerce, growing education, and many impressive technological innovations would require political adaptations. That is why so much was written speculating about the best possible forms of government. Nevertheless, the immediate causes of revolutions were rather more mundane.

The American Revolution began because of a dispute over taxes with the British Parliament. But once under way, it produced a new form of government based largely on English Enlightenment thought. This meant that in principle the rights of all individuals were protected and legitimate government could only come from free elections of representatives who would pass the necessary laws to operate the state. We all know that in practice what occurred was not quite so pure. Slavery was maintained to provide a labor force to grow cotton that met the huge leap in demand from England's textile mills. The writers of the Constitution of the United States knew that with respect to slavery what they were doing violated their principles, and in many cases their writings show that they had a bad conscience about it. Ultimately, this contradiction between crass reality and higher principle caused a great split in the United States and a Civil War from 1860 to 1865 that killed more Americans than any other of its wars.

The enduring problems caused by that original contradiction between principle and the interests of the slave owners should be emphasized, because it brings out the significance of the Enlightenment principles that guided Americans then and now. These principles did not make America perfect, but they caused violations of the principles of democracy to be challenged and provided an abstract model toward which government was supposed to move.

The same has been true in the most democratic western European countries, starting with England and France. It was in these few most advanced Western societies that the almost universal and deeply constraining institutions of agrarian societies—slavery, serfdom, judicial torture, the humiliation of the many by the few, and the reduction of all women to an inferior, servile status—were first brought into question and eventually abolished. The movement throughout the world to abolish these and to make individuals freer is far from complete even to this day, but its impetus still comes out of the West in the late twentieth century.

England was fortunate in that it had maintained an ancient institution from the Middle Ages, a parliament that brought together the various competing elements in society, commoners, lords, the Church, and the king in order to work out their political differences. On the continent of Europe, with the exception of the Netherlands and Sweden, such institutions had been brought under the control of the kings and princes or had simply decayed and become ineffective. In England, however, Parliament provided the basis through which politics could be modernized without revolution, simply by progressively extending the franchise in the nineteenth and through the early twentieth century. In the United States, also, the colonists were used to functioning with English kinds of elected councils and legislatures, and this provided them with a model of how to create their new government after independence.

France was not so fortunate. Its parliamentary institutions had been abolished by its kings in the early seventeenth century, and by the late eighteenth century, when pressures for more representative government forced the king and his ministers to call some sort of assembly together, there were no rules of behavior or parliamentary experience to guide them. The result was a bloody mess in which the various parties, the king, the lords, the Church, and the commoners who wanted more representation maneuvered against each other without knowing how to reach a satisfactory compromise. They wound up fighting a civil war against each other, but the victory of the commoners let loose a reign of terror against the old order and finally a military dictatorship under Napoleon. Imbued with the certitude that French revolutionary principles were just, backed by rising French nationalism, and in command of the most powerful state in Europe, Napoleon tried to conquer the continent. He failed, but introduced the more backward parts of central and southern Europe to the nationalism.

This was only the beginning. After Napoleon's defeat in 1815, the European powers tried to still the revolutionary, nationalist current the French had let loose. They failed because it was too closely tied to the social and economic changes going on in the most successful societies of western Europe, and so it continued to be an example to be followed by the rest of Europe. But the central contradiction of the French revolutionary experience was never resolved. On the one hand revolutionaries were motivated by nationalism, defending the rights of the people of their nation against all others. On the other hand, what this meant in states with several different nationalities, languages, or cultures was that the dominant group felt free to force the others to change and to seize control of the state. So nationalism brought new internal conflicts, new wars over borders, and greater militarization by competing nationalisms. Relying on brute force, persecution of minorities, and the construction of state power for its own sake was the antithesis of the democratization and social progress that Enlightenment thinkers had had in mind.

This contradiction has yet to be resolved. As we saw earlier, with the mixture of nationalism and Darwinian theories of the "survival of the fittest" in the late nineteenth century, nationalist conflicts took on an even more desperate form. Throughout the twentieth century, nationalism has drifted ever further away from the individualistic, liberating ideology it originally embodied and ever more toward its more violent, authoritarian, and intolerant side. The fact that outside a few Western societies nationality has been defined by blood rather than by civic behavior has aggravated this tendency. It has left little room for tolerance or for the gradual assimilation of different groups into the nation.

Industrialization produced another new ideology in the nineteenth century, socialism. The principal idea behind socialism is simple, and it has already been discussed. Capitalism is based on self-interest and greed, and therefore, say socialists, it is morally inferior to communal forms of organization that take into consideration the general welfare over that of individuals. Furthermore, basing action on higher considerations than pure self-interest is presumed to yield a more humane type of society.

There were many different forms of socialism. At one extreme anarchists believed that destroying the state would automatically liquidate capitalism and social injustice. People would spontaneously form themselves into cooperative associations and work out their own problems. This was their rationale for assassinating heads of state and other powerful people. The idea was that if only a few such people were removed, the rest of society would rid itself of the state and oppressive private property rules.

More realistic socialists, however, recognized that eliminating a few people at the top was unlikely to bring about fundamental change. Revolutionary organization was necessary in order to bring about the systematic conquest of power. Socialist ideas were developed primarily by intellectuals who found capitalist bourgeois life unfair, dull, and crass; but they needed troops to back them, and these they hoped to find in the growing class of factory workers. Indeed, as industrialization advanced, workers learned to become better organized in unions and socialist parties. By the late nineteenth century socialist parties representing the workers' interests had become a significant force in Germany, France, England, and the other advanced European countries. In the United States, which lacked a socialist party, the unions and the urban wing of the Democratic Party served the same purpose.

From the point of view of true revolutionaries, however, this was not satisfactory, because the stronger the workers became the more they insisted on using their influence to obtain better wages and working conditions. As capitalism was an engine for producing ever greater amounts of wealth, it was possible for the owners and managers of enterprises to pay ever higher wages to the workers and satisfy their demands. Unions and democratic socialist parties thus became less revolutionary and more practical. For intellectuals who loathed the very idea of capitalism this was treachery, and they remained unhappy with the "corruption" of unions and democratic socialist parties.

In Russia and other backward societies that began their industrialization only in the very late nineteenth or in the twentieth century, revolutionary intellectuals were better able to recruit substantial numbers of workers and discontented peasants to their cause because the standard of living remained low and inequality higher than in more advanced societies. Thus in Russia the revolutionary Marxists led by Lenin were more successful than their extremist counterparts in England, France, Germany, or the United States. This pattern would be reproduced elsewhere later in the twentieth century. Marxist revolutions that led to communism wound up taking place only in newly industrializing, relatively backward societies: China, Vietnam, Yugoslavia, and Cuba. Marx's prediction that socialist revolutions would take place in the most advanced economies proved to be wrong.

But the revolutionary Marxists left a very deep imprint on the twentieth century despite the inaccuracy of Marx's predictions. In 1917 Lenin's party seized power in Russia and set up the world's first communist state, the Soviet Union, which would become the world's second greatest power and last for seventy-four years. In the 1920s the Chinese Communist Party was formed, and after a long, bloody series of civil wars, it took power in 1949. With the occupation of Eastern Europe by the Soviet Union after World War II and the triumph of communism in China, by 1950 Marxist communists ruled one third of the globe.

The appeal of Marxism was that it promised equality and the end of the alienation supposedly produced by capitalism. But since it was more successful in relatively backward societies, the first item on its agenda in the twentieth century was to modernize the economy, industrialize, and strengthen the state in order to preserve the gains of communism against hostile and advanced capitalist powers.

The Marxist vision of history as a matter of unending and fierce class struggle that was bound to lead to revolution and the sense of isolation in a capitalist world produced a sense in all communist societies that they were under perpetual siege from internal and external enemies. This resulted in ruthless dictatorships that justified their execution of millions of class enemies, the mass confiscation of property, and the militarization of society by an appeal to the ultimate, utopian principles of socialism. Because the ultimate goal was to return to a kind of Garden of Eden, and because the propertied classes of the world were presented as demons out to stop progress, any means were considered justified to carry out the revolution. Also, since industrial backwardness weakened these societies, they had to force huge investments out of their people in order to catch up. This meant that ever more force had to be used to deprive people of consumption goods, to take food and land away from recalcitrant peasants, to prevent strikes by workers, and to prevent the discontented professionals in the middle class from fleeing.

It all worked up to a point. Factories were built, most communist societies were substantially industrialized and modernized, and the biggest ones, Russia and China, became great world powers. The military success and power of communist states managed for a time to capture the sense of nationalism in their societies. Communism promised to make backward nations catch up to the powerful West. It was based on ideas that claimed to be scientific, but that rejected free market, individualistic capitalism. This was more congenial to non-Western societies than Western liberal ideology, but it avoided the danger of remaining too traditional.

But by centralizing economic control into the hands of communist parties and an elite of planners, communism created an unworkable system. Lenin, his successor Stalin, Mao Zedong in China, and other early communist leaders based their model of an advanced industrial society on what they learned about the advanced West during the third industrial cycle. They applied force to create the same conditions: giant steel mills, huge electrification projects, extreme concentration of capital and workers in giant factories, and an emphasis on goods that were used to build more factories instead of consumer goods. But such centralization worked less well in the fourth industrial cycle which required the production of consumer goods and much greater sensitivity to consumer demands. No communist economy ever fully mastered the technology and innovative drive of the fourth industrial cycle. Finally, none could cope at all with the fifth cycle.

In the age of electronics and biotechnology extreme flexibility is required. Not only free thought to allow scientific innovation but also good marketing that allows a firm to adapt quickly to changes in demand are necessary. No highly centralized, planned economy could hope to achieve this as quickly as a decentralized economy used to dealing with free markets.

Communist economies, even the most advanced, never caught up to the foremost Western industrial economies. By the fifth industrial age, they were falling behind quickly. Not only that, but the relatively free market economies of East Asia, starting with Japan and followed by Taiwan, South Korea, Hong Kong, and Singapore, proved to be far more adaptable than the communists in making progress. It became obvious that the oppression and suffering imposed by communists on their people were not leading to faster progress and that the possibility of achieving a socialist utopia was becoming more remote. Communist elites lost faith in themselves.

The collapse of communism in Eastern Europe and the Soviet Union from 1989 to 1991 proves that no matter how powerful a modern state, in the long run it must rest on a certain degree of ideological legitimacy. Democratic capitalism provides this through the ideas of the Enlightenment. Communism based its legitimacy on the predictions of Marx. When these turned out to be empty, the system rotted from within and fell.

The other major anticapitalist ideology in the modern era has been fascism. Though fascism is supposed to be "right wing" and communism "left wing," and though they have been hostile to each other, the two ideologies have much in common. Fascism was also primarily the creation of intellectuals hostile to European bourgeois culture, to democracy, and to capitalism. It sought to return to a more heroic and less crassly materialistic age, to eliminate the alienation of modern society, and to recreate communal bonds. But unlike socialism it did not promise to return to the equality of preagrarian societies. Instead, it sought to revive the institutions of agrarian societies in which everyone had a place and the strong led the way.

At its most creative, fascism came up with the idea of corporatism. All social groups would be organized in something resembling medieval guilds, protective associations that would represent their members and protect their interests. But instead of being based on class, with the working class and capitalists being hostile to each other, fascist corporations were going to be based on the branch of activity from which people gained their livelihood. Thus factory workers and managers in a given industry would be in the same corporation. All people in agriculture would be in a common corporation, as would those in education, or creative artists. Above this structure there would be a grand arbitrator, a council of corporation representatives led by the supreme leader of the state and his ruling party, to adjudicate between conflicting claims of corporations.

In practice, this system is surprisingly similar to what communist societies worked out for themselves. It also suffered from many of the same problems, particularly excess centralization, dictatorship, and the corruption of unchecked power that allowed those in charge to exploit their positions for personal gain at the expense of the general welfare.

After the collapse of the main fascist powers at the end of World War II, most advanced capitalist societies adopted some corporatist principles. The idea that mediation between interest groups had to be enforced by a strong state, that social institutions that protected communal relations and could override market forces were necessary, and that an impartial state bureaucracy that stood above politics was necessary to make modern society work became widely accepted in western Europe and Japan, though somewhat less in the United States.

Fascism in the early twentieth century, however, developed another trait which was far less benign than the ideal of corporatism. The idealization of heroism and brute strength over the rational, petty calculations of the bourgeoisie fit very well with grand ideas of nationalism. In the case of German and Japanese fascism these ideas were combined with a sense that their nations were racially superior. Nationalism mixed in with a popularized, simplified version of Darwinism and an admiration for brute strength and heroism led the fascist powers into great wars of conquest. This was the main cause of World War II, and it was only their military defeat that caused the term *fascism* to fall into such disrepute. Yet the fascist critique of democratic bourgeois society continues to appeal to many intellectuals, as well as to leaders in poorer countries who are still looking for ways to catch up to the West without having to adopt the same ideologies of democracy, individualism, and the free market.

There is little doubt that in the late twentieth century the collapse of communism and the decline of socialist idealism will once again give strength to those critics of capitalism who lean toward fascist solutions. In fact, the spread of bitterly anti-Western religious movements throughout some poor parts of the world, particularly among Islamic nations, is creating a new version of fascism, but one that relies on many of the same ideas of communal solidarity, heroism, and anti-Enlightenment intolerance as the earlier fascisms of the twentieth century.

Both fascism and socialism had more than certain organizing principles in common. They rejected the liberal assumption that somehow free markets, that is, purely impersonal, undirected economic mechanisms, were really capable of solving the economic crises engendered by the industrial age. What socialism tried to overcome by more rational planning and internationalist appeals to working class interests, fascism sought to overcome by rebuilding the bonds of a supposed racial community and destroying the crass materialism of bourgeois capitalism. Both aimed to rebuild a sense of supposedly lost communal solidarity.

Socialism and fascism in power disappointed many of their followers because of the necessary compromises forced on them by having to rule real countries. But the ideals remained important, first as blueprints for the future and second as motivating myths that could energize true believers.

Fascism and socialism have had a particularly strong appeal in those societies that considered themselves backward or relatively weak compared to the most successful and powerful capitalist states. They both offered the promise of being uniquely able to solve the problem of backwardness by invigorating the economy, building national strength, and at the same time resisting the pernicious influence of the most powerful capitalist democracies.

In conclusion, then, three great revolutionary ideologies have dominated the modern era: Enlightenment liberalism, socialism, and fascism.

The first, which emphasizes individual rights against the state, the importance of democracy, and the need to let the economy be regulated by markets, has come out the winner. Socialism sprang originally from the Enlightenment but abandoned the idea of individual rights and tried to plan economic growth. It failed in the late twentieth century. Fascism, which began as an anti-Enlightenment ideology, led the world to the greatest war it has ever known at mid-century, and has been in relative eclipse since then.

But Enlightenment liberalism has its problems, too. It has fostered nationalism, which can easily be accommodated by both the extreme left and right and which continues to cause violent conflict. It has encouraged scientific advances that are generally misunderstood by most people and turn into extremist, pseudoscientific excuses for bloody tyranny such as Soviet communism or German fascism. And it has led to an economic system that, for all its success, goes from one cyclical crisis to the next and leaves unsolved the problems of internal and international inequality. Therefore it would be difficult to predict that the age of revolutions and political unrest that began in the late eighteenth century is really over or that the twenty-first century will see the peaceful spread of democratic capitalism without international or internal social conflicts.

War, Tyranny, and the Success of Western Enlightenment Values

The modern era has experienced so many and such rapid changes in two centuries that it is easy to think that the rules of social and cultural evolution no longer apply. To believe this is as foolish as to believe that because human beings are far smarter than other mammals they have escaped the rules of biological evolution.

Certain habits, social structures, and ideologies are better adapted to the modern world than others, and as our social, economic, and political environment change so quickly, what worked well at one time may no longer be as suitable a short time later. Western European societies became rich and powerful because they allowed their intellectuals greater freedom to explore new ideas, because towns were more independent, and because commercial rationality became a more important part of social life than elsewhere. Westerners developed new religious ideas that emphasized the rational pursuit of truth by each individual instead of mere acceptance of ancient dogmas; and they pioneered the idea that individual rights had to be protected against state power. The democratic political organization of the most successful Western states, their inventiveness in science and technology, and their successful industrialization all flowed from these attributes. Together, they formed the basis of a liberal world view that within two hundred years created greater prosperity and a freer environment for the inhabitants of advanced societies than anything which had existed in agrarian societies.

During much of the twentieth century it seemed that the liberal, bourgeois, democratic, and capitalist view of the world was obsolete and that it would be replaced by more efficient, more ruthless, and more communal ideologies, fascism and communism. In the end, however, these antiliberal ways of thought built monstrous tyrannies that provoked wars and repression on an unprecedented scale. In their search for racial purity German fascists, the Nazis, murdered ten million people, of whom six million were Jews, and started a war that killed another twenty million. The Japanese invaded and brutalized China in the 1930s and then set out to conquer Southeast Asia. At least twenty-five million died as a result of this. In the Soviet Union, Stalin's policies that were supposed to bring about socialism resulted in the murder and forced starvation of at least ten million peasants, and in the political purges, deportations to forced labor camps, and mass shootings that followed at least another ten to fifteen million were killed. In Mao's China at least thirty million and perhaps far more were starved to death or murdered, or died in prison camps as part of the attempt to create socialism. In Cambodia, in four years, from 1975 to 1979, a communist government killed close to one fifth of the entire population in order to create a purer society devoted to communal values and to purify the Cambodia race by eliminating Vietnamese, Chinese, and other minorities.

Every government in the twentieth century run according to the major anti-Enlightenment, antiliberal principles that have formed the backbone of protest against Western democratic capitalism has been a murderous tyranny that has brought its people war, economic ruin, and ultimate destruction. This has been true of regimes as different from each other as that in South Africa which enforced racial separation from the 1940s to the early 1990s, Mussolini's fascist government in Italy from 1922 to 1943, the supposedly egalitarian and progressive communist government of North Korea, and the nationalist and isolationist "Buddhist socialist" regime of Ne Win in Burma from 1962 into the 1990s. Nor have the Western democracies escaped the consequences when they have betrayed their own principles by trying to maintain foreign colonies. These colonial empires, built largely in the late nineteenth century when social Darwinism was at its height, ended in the mid-twentieth century, often through bitter wars, especially in Africa and Southeast Asia.

This is, after all is said and done, a proof that the cultural traits that have been best adapted to the modern world have been those produced by the democratic and liberal Western heirs to the Enlightenment. When the British and French were forced to give up their colonies and adhere to the political philosophy that made them democratic and successful in the first place, their societies benefited. When the Germans or Japanese had these values forced on them, as they were after World War II, they prospered and were freed from the tyrannies that had ruled them.

But though this should be a comfort to the world, because it suggests that by adopting and adapting to Western cultures and practices it is possible to modernize successfully, it would be a mistake to believe that the future necessarily will flow in that direction. First of all, in the poorer parts of the world, there is continuing hostility and jealousy against the prosperous societies in the world. Their intellectuals and leaders admired communism as long as it held out any prospect of overcoming the West, and more recently these societies have experienced extremely angry movements that so loathe Western Enlightenment culture that they cannot accept its main principles.

Second, throughout the world there is nationalism that brought the most advanced nations to war against each other in the early twentieth century, and this could happen again. Third, even within the most advanced Western nations there remain many discontented intellectuals spinning out theories of why capitalism, liberalism, and individualism are evil and should be opposed by antimarket, communal values that would glorify non-Western cultures and renounce everything that has been achieved in the recent past. To be sure, such intellectuals are not likely to have much of an audience in good times. But in moments of crisis, when industrial cycles are shifting, when old centers of prosperity are declining and being replaced by new ones, when some previously strong nations are losing ground to others and competition is increasing, then such ideologies of resentment will thrive and gain political converts. This is what happened as a result of the chaos of World War I, when from 1917 to 1939 most of Europe became fascist or communist. It happened again in the chaos after World War II when communism made such immense gains.

Finally, an even greater reason for doubting that the future will unfold in the same direction as the recent past is that the conditions that originally produced the modernizing impulse in the West are now long gone. In a very crowded, wealthy world, new types of organization and new ideologies may be necessary to adapt successfully. We will touch on this briefly in the next section of this chapter, and in the book's conclusions.

Ideologies are like the genes that shape cultures and societies. They provide the blueprints from which realities are constructed. Most of the new ideological movements brought up by modernization have been neither benign nor adaptive; yet they have been strong enough to rule large parts of the world and almost take it over. We can never be certain that this will not happen again or, for that matter, that the most successful, adaptive cultures of the past two centuries will not themselves succumb as they change and lose their original principles and vigor.

Ecological Pressures Persist

In the late twentieth century the general public has become aware of the global strain on resources, wildlife, air, and water caused by industrialization. We know, of course, that the interaction between human beings and their environment has repeatedly caused ecological stress in the past.

There were many preindustrial examples of overuse that resulted in severe problems. North American hunters exterminated many of the largest species of mammals after migrating into the continent from Asia during the last ice age. Middle Eastern civilizations caused excess salinity of their fields by irrigating them too much. Nomads from Arabia destroyed agricultural productivity in North Africa by bringing in too many sheep and goats and overgrazing the land. The ancient population cycle in agrarian societies was an almost inevitable by-product of the interaction between humans and their environment, and there was no permanent solution to this recurring ecological problem before the technological progress made by industrial societies.

The ecological problems caused by the interaction between industrial societies and the environment, therefore, are a continuation of a very old pattern that has in the past only been solved by new technological advances. New advances that will solve present problems will undoubtedly create new ecological problems we cannot even foresee. The idea that some present ecological crisis can be remedied by returning to old ways is false because to do this would only bring back some previously solved crisis, except that with the human population so much greater than it was in the past, any attempt to reimpose agrarian cultures on the world would result in an even more massive agrarian demographic catastrophe than any in the past.

We can be quite certain that because climatic changes occurred in the past, they will continue to take place in the future. Global heating and cooling have come and gone, sometimes in just a few centuries, and these contributed to agrarian population cycles as well. But again, adaptable human cultures have managed to thrive despite these changes, and can again. Failure to adapt for some societies, now as before, will mean massive suffering and death, while successful social change will propel the most flexible and innovative cultures to new levels.

This is not the place to catalogue the strains on the earth and on human populations created by the huge increases in productivity and population over the past two hundred years. Nor would it be very useful to speculate about what technological and scientific solutions will be found to solve these pressures, much less about the inevitable new problems that will be created by these solutions. Nevertheless, some generalizations based on our general knowledge of past social change are in order.

The greatest danger is not that present ecological problems are impossible to solve, but that the cultural forces that oppose continued modernization will be politically triumphant. If this were to happen in the most developed industrial societies, as it happened in the past in some of the most advanced agrarian societies like ancient Egypt or China in the Middle Ages, who then will take the role of bringing about the necessary progress and pushing forward social evolution?

We can guess that in the future, as in the past, certain societies will be more innovative than others. Some have organizations that adapt more quickly than others. Will the tighter, more corporatist social structure of Japan turn out to be more adaptable than the more individualistic and decentralized form of organization in the United States? Will societies where population continues to grow very quickly be able to compete more successfully in a crowded world than the rich, industrialized societies with low birth rates?

Past experience suggests that new solutions will come from the most flexible, less tradition-bound, more secular, and less centralized societies. For one thing, in such societies highly motivated, somewhat marginal migrant or "stranger" subcultures who have fled from bad conditions in their homelands have the opportunity to put their talents and energies to use. This is why migrating Chinese throughout the world but especially in Southeast Asia have been economically and culturally more dynamic than those in China itself, and why certain small minority populations who are considered strangers—for example, Jews and Armenians in Europe and America or East Indians emigrants in many parts of the world—have played such an important role in promoting economic and cultural progress. Then too, more open societies are more tolerant of new ideas and less likely to impose conformity. It is from the nonconformists, from those who are different, from those who do not blindly follow the conventions of the majority, that there come fresh ideas that provide the blueprints for social evolution and adaptation.

Certainly, as far as the environmental problems of industrial societies are concerned, we know that the highly centralized, most advanced communist economies did a much worse job than the advanced capitalist ones. We also know that the United States, which is the most decentralized of the big, advanced industrial societies and the one most ruled by market forces, has been more innovative in pioneering solutions to such problems than others.

The past suggests that humans are not about to run out of solutions to their environmental and ecological problems as long as innovation is not crushed by overly powerful states that impose cultural uniformity and orthodoxy. Resources need not be exhausted if prices are allowed to rise as they become scarce. Then new technologies will be found that use different resources or save in the use of old ones. In the agrarian age it was not just because technology was primitive that ecological catastrophes occurred, but also because free movement of peasants was generally not allowed, because new ideas for organizing production were not considered valid, and because in times of crisis societies became more conservative. Economic systems driven by the market receive signals that something is going wrong much earlier than do those ruled primarily by political forces and ideology.

In the modern era the most successful industrial societies have built ever stronger states. We know that when agrarian societies did this, it led, eventually, to stagnation and a failure to adapt. Will this pattern be repeated? It could be, of course, and this would place the entire human race in serious jeopardy. But if the most modern, most advanced societies retain open, tolerant political and social systems, they will retain their capacity to innovate and adapt. In other words, if they continue to replicate some of the conditions that led to the great scientific and technological progress made in the past few centuries, then there is no reason to be pessimistic about the future. But if these conditions are curtailed, there will be few grounds for being optimistic.

Reference Notes
(Full references are in the bibliography)

Eric Hobsbawm's three volumes *The Age of Revolution, The Age of Capital,* and *The Age of Empire* are the most lively and theoretically informed social, political, and economic histories of how Europe changed from the late eighteenth to the early twentieth century. Hobsbawm is also the world's most sophisticated living Marxist historian, and though Marxism is in a state of general decline, his books will remain classics in the twenty-first century because they are so balanced and convincing.

Karl Marx himself left a huge opus. His *Early Writings* contain his most provocative philosophical speculations, centered especially on his attempt to understand the nature of alienation in modern society. The first and key volume of *Capital*, written much later, includes his most developed economic theorizing and a lot of examples that explain the causes and consequences of the rise of capitalism. Marx, however, is not easy to read. Hobsbawm uses the same ideas but in a more subtle and comprehensible way, and also includes accounts of twentieth-century historical research that require modification of Marx's original theories.

Joseph Schumpeter's collected essays are required reading for anyone who wishes to understand the nature of capitalism, both its strengths and its weaknesses. Karl Polanyi's *The Great Transformation*, written in the early 1940s, is still the most persuasive theoretical critique of full market capitalism and its potential for destroying agrarian societies, with sometimes catastrophic consequences. Barrington Moore's *The Social Origins of Dictatorship and Democracy* traces the origins of the twentieth century's most destructive revolutionary ideologies as well as of Western democracies back to the ways in which societies originally modernized their economies at the start of the Industrial Revolution, or, in non-European cases, as a result of contact with the West.

The idea of industrial cycles based on technological change owes much to David Landes, whose *Unbound Prometheus* meticulously details the connection between science, technology, and economy during the first two centuries of the industrial age. Walt Rostow's *The World Economy* presents vast amounts of data to support the notion of regular economic cycles. In an earlier book on social change, *Social Change in the Modern Era*, I used these works and those of other economic historians to spell out in more detail than in the present book the nature and social consequences of these cycles. Charles Kindleberger's economic history of the Great Depression of the 1930s, *The World in Depression*, is the most readable and in many ways the most believable account of the consequences of one such cycle. It shows that although disruptive changes would have created economic problems in any case, these were greatly aggravated by policy errors and poor economic theory.

The philosophical and historical origins of Enlightenment liberalism are discussed for the United States in Bernard Baylin's *The Ideological Origins of the American Revolution.* Isaiah Berlin, one of the world's foremost political philosophers, makes the nature of modern liberalism, both its benefits and its potential for turning into something sinister, clearer in his *Four Essays on Liberty.* Such works can be demanding, but they get beyond the simplistic propaganda that too often passes for political thought these days.

The awful consequences of anti-Enlightenment political thought, many of them coming out of misguided attempts to overcome the problems of industrial society, are spelled out in my recent book *Modern Tyrants.* H. Stuart Hughes's *Consciousness and Society* explains in great detail how the revolt against the simplifying scientific assumptions of nineteenth-century liberalism led to advances in social theory but also to the development of communism and especially fascism. More specifically, to learn about fascism, it is hardly possible to do better than to read the essays in the work edited by Hans Rogger and Eugen Weber, *The European Right.*

The seeming success and eventual failure of communism, particularly in Russia, have to be understood by students of social change because the collapse of communism has been the most important global development in the late twentieth century. The best introduction to modern Russian history is found in the succinct and elegant collected essays of Leonard Schapiro, *Russian Studies.* Geoffrey Hosking's *The Awakening of the Soviet Union* is the most convincing account of what happened there to lead to such a spectacular fall. Kenneth Jowitt's *The Leninist Response to National Dependency* is a welcome reminder that originally the popularity of communism in poor societies was not as irrational as it now seems to be in light of recent events.

Understanding industrial societies, and why some succeed so well while others do not, requires some knowledge of basic facts about such things as rates of economic and demographic growth and income distribution. No source is better than the annual volumes put out by the World Bank in their *World Development Reports.*

All students, but especially ones from the U.S., need to know that the American model has not been the only or in some aspects even the most successful one in the world. Peter Katzenstein's *Corporatism and Change* looks at some small European societies to show that they have both controlled their capitalism more than Americans and also achieved a greater level of social equality. Chalmers Johnson's study of *MITI and the Japanese Miracle* presents a very different kind of capitalism than the one Americans are used to. A high degree of social consensus and of government interference have made Japan more competitive, not less so. Many of the same lessons can be learned from Ezra Vogel's superb short study on the causes of success in four little East Asian societies that have had the highest growth rates in the world in the late twentieth century (*The Four Little Dragons*).

Though many economists do not take John Kenneth Galbraith seriously, he is always provocative, his irony can be a relief after one has read too many pompous academic tomes, and he is usually more right than his critics. His *The New Industrial State* was a prediction about the nature of social stratification in a future high-tech world. Though his scenario has not yet come to pass, at least not fully, it may. One thing he makes clear is that education and the dissemination of knowledge are going to be growth industries for a long time to come, and those who control them will wield increasing power.

5

Toward a Theory of Social Change

Throughout this book I have been using an implicit model of how societies work. It is time to make it explicit. This model is based on a complicated general theory of society worked out in the 1950s by the American sociologist Talcott Parsons. Parsons went further than any other twentieth-century social theorist in systematically exploring the relationship between economies, political systems, different types of social institutions, and cultures. He also combined an extensive knowledge of history with an awareness of the analogies between social systems and biological organisms. Greatly simplified and somewhat modified for the sake of clarity, his theoretical model, which follows, offers us a useful way of approaching the study of social change.

There are four analytically distinct aspects or subsystems of all human societies: the economy, the political system, social institutions, and culture.

The economy interacts directly with the environment. It is in this sphere of activity that humans work to produce what they need. But economies do not operate in a vacuum. Various societies organize their economic lives very differently depending on their technologies, goals, ways of organizing themselves, and ultimate values.

Decisions about power—determining how production is to be organized and its fruits distributed, who gets what, and who orders whom around—are made by the political system. This is where decisions are made about how to achieve the goals of the society. Thus the invention of the state created that institution which even now, five thousand years later, is the ultimate decision-making, political authority for almost all human beings. It is the state that decides what type of economic system will prevail. For example, communist states in the twentieth century used much the same technology as capitalist states, and production methods were quite similar. But the political and social distribution of power, the social consequences of production, and the uses to which it was put were different. Politics and economics interact in ways that make it impossible for either social subsystem to be independent of the other.

There is another level of social organization that consists of the actual institutions in which we live. All societies more complicated than the earliest band of hunters and gatherers lived within many varied institutional constraints, and the number of these has increased. Thousands of types of social institutions exist. We may belong to a few or to many of them, but almost all of us belong to at least several. We perform economic functions in institutional settings that vary from very large firms or bureaucratic organizations to the tiny firm or the family. The state is our primary political institution, but there are many other institutional levels below the state that are also involved with politics: parties, local administrative bodies, organized pressure groups, and so on. Much of what satisfaction we may derive from our lives is derived from our participation in various institutional groups: families, clubs, churches, sororities, groups of entertainers we may watch or belong to, and the like, as well as informal groups that can become similar to institutions, such as bands of friends. Then there are institutions that preserve our culture, educate us, and give meaning to our lives, such as schools, churches, museums, newspapers, or radio talk shows we listen to and call.

The final social subsystem is what has so far in this book been called *culture*. This contains the codes or blueprints of social systems. Cultures interpret our surroundings for us and give them meaning and allow us to express ourselves. Languages, religions, science, art, notions of right and wrong, explanations of the meaning of life—these are all part of the cultural system of a society.

Obviously the various parts of the social system interact and could not, in fact, exist alone. Yet even though separating these parts for purpose of analysis is an artificial exercise, much of the disagreement between different types of specialists who study societies comes from the fact that by concentrating on one or another of its distinct subsystems, they forget that what they are looking at cannot exist in isolation. Economists who believe that all societies are governed by the laws of the market make the error of forgetting that in many cases—for example, the classical agrarian societies—political will and cultural value systems overrode the forces of the market. In the twentieth century, much of the gigantic effort made by communist societies to impose order on their people was deliberately designed to counter markets. This made economies far less efficient and flexible than they could have been, but the force of traditional and political will may be strong enough to cause stagnation and poverty for very long periods of time. At the same time, preserving a market-oriented economy requires noneconomic values and institutions that preserve the market against those who want to curb it for moral or esthetic reasons.

Similarly, sociologists who tend to emphasize social institutions such as families or neighborhoods tend to forget that economic pressures and changing ideas are really the main causes of change. Institutions as such, the concrete ways people have of organizing their daily lives, do not determine the essential direction of social change.

Marxism, which was a powerful social theory, perhaps the single most powerful from the 1920s until the 1980s, concentrated on the interaction between economic and political systems and institutions, but neglected the cultural part of the society. Thus for Marxists ideas were only representations of economic and political interests and had no particular meaning on their own. Yet Marxism in its political form, as the ideology that produced governments in the Soviet Union, China, and many other countries, or that animated various types of socialist parties elsewhere, was itself an idea, a faith that repeatedly ignored economic realities in order to carry out a kind of religious mission. The idea of egalitarian socialism created a political will that in turn created economic and social institutions rather than the other way around.

But even those who study cultures make the same error of forgetting other parts of the social system. Ideas are only codes. They are in a sense like genetic codes: From them come actual social institutions. But neither societies nor human beings are infinitely flexible. There are biological imperatives that come from the need for survival, and these force human beings into certain sorts of economic and institutional arrangements that cannot be altered without threatening the survival of the entire society. We do not just invent ourselves as we may wish.

New ideas about how to live and what goals we wish to achieve as societies may be tried, but then they are tested and succeed or fail according to how well they allow societies to adapt. What goes for whole social systems applies also to the smaller institutions within a society. These too are subjected to continual testing. Only a few innovations survive long; most that are tried are either insignificant or failures.

A good example is the fact that human societies cannot do without family structures. Those that try are doomed because children are raised inadequately. This has not prevented many different types of experiments from being tried, ranging from sects that thought they could survive without sexual reproduction (an obvious dead end) to whole societies that tried to remove children from their biological parents and raise them communally. There are considerable differences in family structure from society to society, and it is possible for people to reproduce physically without family support, but so far no way has been found to reproduce a functioning social system without families.

Similarly, human societies cannot eliminate competition, inequality of talent, and the basic need to engage in some sort of struggle to survive. There have been ideologies that have tried to do away with inequality and competition, just as there have been some that have wanted to do away with families. When put into practice, they have all failed.

Furthermore, at any given technological level, there are certain requirements that must be met. For example, no industrial society can function without a complicated school system. No modern society can succeed without ample funding for scientific research. It is possible to try to reduce the expenses for education or for research, but long before these fall to zero, there will be severe consequences and disaster.

What this means is that in order to understand how societies work and change we must first be able to say under what conditions innovation takes place. Second, we have to be able to understand why certain innovations work and others do not, and why, over time, what may have worked in the past ceases to work so well in the present. Understanding biological evolution requires a similar kind of dual analysis: what causes genetic change and what works or does not.

In the case of social change, we have to analyze the causes and consequences of change in terms of the various social subsystems: economies, political systems, social institutions or organizations, and cultures.

The two most interesting parts of the social system are the part that interacts with natural world, the economy, and the part that provides the codes that shape social systems, the culture. The former is the ultimate test of how adequately a society is responding to various ecological exigencies, and it is within the latter that "mutations," new ideas, occur for meeting challenges.

Cultural innovation includes, of course, technological and scientific discoveries that make economic progress possible. Yet as the pressures for change reverberate throughout a social system, the system adjusts and tries to accommodate without altering either its social institutions or its way of conducting politics. Thus we find in most societies that actual institutions and the political system resist changes that originate in material exigencies or cultural innovation. This opens an ever increasing gap between material or ideological pressures and institutional forms. This gap may become so large as to cause sudden and major breaks with the past as social institutions finally crack and either remold themselves to accommodate the pressures for change that have been building up or fail and drag down the entire society. It is during these revolutionary, dramatic times that the rate of social change occurs most quickly. It is also the way in which social institutions resist change that accounts for the discontinuous rate of change: long periods of relative stability followed by sudden, wrenching adjustments.

The collapse of European communism in the late twentieth century is a good example. Strains built up as a result of poor economic performance and growing dissidence. People ceased to believe in the validity of Marxist ideology. Yet the system carried on, trying to maintain the same institutions and political system, until finally it cracked. By then slow change was no longer possible and the political death of communism was followed by a series of dramatic economic depressions, wars, and grave social turmoil.

Why Change Occurs

There are two sets of ways in which complex, large societies receive information about how well they are doing. One is based on comparisons with other societies, and the other is internal.

One type of signal that informs a society that it is not functioning well is that neighboring societies become stronger and defeat it in war. This was usually the principal way agrarian societies had of telling that something was wrong. Though society and state are not identical, the governors of the state assumed responsibility for their society and judged their success by how well they did in competition with their neighbors. The states that conquered neighbors and grew deemed that they ruled over successful social systems. Severe losses, on the other hand, brought about self-doubt and opened the way for attempts at change.

Another external signal that something is wrong is when the economic performance of other societies is superior to one's own. This raises questions about why one's society is not operating as well as possible. In practice, it has only been very recently, in the industrial age, that this kind of comparison has become possible. In the United States today, for example, there is much speculation about why Japan seems to be a better ordered, commercially more dynamic society than the United States. It has not taken a military defeat by Japan to make the United States think about reform, though of course there is no guarantee that without a major catastrophe there will be meaningful reform.

In agrarian economies economic statistics were not gathered, practically all peasants lived miserably, and very few people traveled enough between different societies to tell which one was doing better, much less why. Therefore, as far as external signals are concerned, until the nineteenth century or even the twentieth, war was almost the only mechanism for testing how well a social system was functioning.

Internal signals could also be economic or political. Periods of starvation, which could lead to actual extinction of a whole society in pre-agrarian small groups, were unlikely to produce total collapse in an agrarian society. But bleak episodes of economic failure invariably resulted in massive disruptions, internal war, and suffering such that societies received the signal that something was wrong. But again, economic failure was poorly understood and often ascribed to divine displeasure or the personal moral failings of the rulers. It was unlikely to cause profound changes in how society was organized because it did not make elites want to resign their high positions; nor was there much opportunity to find other, new ways of organizing societies. So internal economic disruption, when it led to change, usually did so through civil war of one kind or another, or quite often through a combination of internal war and invasion from the outside.

In modern industrial societies with good economic statistics and a high level of education it is possible for people to judge their relative success or failure by seeing how their economies perform, but without experiencing massive economic collapses. Presumably in democracies where political performance is constantly being monitored and judged by the society as a whole, it is even easier to respond to unfavorable economic news with a change of policy. Indeed, this is one of the paradoxes of modern social change. Highly advanced, industrialized, democratic societies, which seem so prone to rapid change and sudden shifts in public opinion, turn out to be able to manage change more successfully than more rigid agrarian societies of the past or highly centralized, nondemocratic modern ones.

Even in the twentieth century, great social experiments, such as the attempt to set up fascist systems, failed through war, not by peacefully examining relative degrees of economic well-being. Japan and Germany, so successful in the late twentieth century as democratic, capitalist societies, had major changes forced on them after 1945 only because they had been defeated in history's biggest war. In the case of the communist collapse, a critical factor was that the military leadership in the Soviet Union began to see that it was falling seriously behind the West in the arms race because its modern technology and economic power were inadequate. War, or the capacity to make war successfully, remains a key indicator of a society's ability to survive, though not always the main one as it used to be.

What if in the past there had been societies without war, without social unrest, with no shifts due to rising population, and without ecological pressures of some kind? We know the answer to this because even though such perfection was never reached, in some cases something close to it was obtained. Ancient Egypt was relatively so successful that it stagnated and ceased to change. Though China was hardly a perfect society in the Middle Ages, it solved its problems so well that it stagnated compared to Europe. Similarly, preagrarian peoples who learned to control their population growth and to live in harmony with their environment did not change until they ran into more aggressive, more trouble-prone social systems that then overcame them. But then they were likely to be threatened with rapid annihilation.

We can be sure that without pressures of some kind there would be virtually no social change. We also know that pressures manifest themselves as failures, and that until very recently, signals indicating failure always took very unpleasant forms. Though it is now possible to respond to economic signals, either internal or external, it may still be necessary in most cases for wars or other catastrophes, at least massive economic depressions, to take place before fundamental changes occur.

Using the model elaborated in the first part of this chapter, we can see how pressures for change produce a response. Cultures—that is, ideas about what is right and wrong, as well as knowledge about the environment—are always changing. It is a human tendency for those with enough time to think to speculate about the meaning of their lives and their environment and about how best to organize social life. The urge to be inventive and find new technologies is as powerful. Many strange proposals for social change and impractical technologies have been thought up and few have been carried out. But when the external environment, through either economic or political signals, through internal failures or the greater success of outsiders, informs a society that something is going wrong, it is from the repertoire of available suggestions for change that reform actually comes about.

Western Europe did not change so quickly in the nineteenth century just because of the preceding several centuries of scientific and philosophical change. But the presence of a vast accumulation of ideas made extremely rapid adaptation possible when economic and political pressures appeared to push European societies out of the agrarian era. Non-European societies, even the most advanced such as China, did not have such a store of models available until they learned about Western science and social organization. But once such learning had taken place, even though it was only among a rather small number of intellectuals, change in non-Western societies could take place very rapidly.

It took less than a century for the Chinese to discover that their ancient system, so well adapted to meeting the competition from other agrarian states and overcoming periodic internal ecological crises, was entirely inadequate in facing the threat from modern Europe. Then it took much discussion among Chinese intellectuals, fighting between various political factions, and experimenting with different types of administration over about eight decades for China to begin to come up with the required changes. These issues are still far from settled in contemporary China, and many old religious attitudes and moral ideals have not changed. But the economy is organized differently, the political system no longer works the way the old imperial system did, and most of all, Chinese intellectual life has been revolutionized by the introduction of modern science and political philosophy. This vast reservoir of new ideas makes it certain that in the future social institutions will continue to change and have an adequate store of models to use in order to continue to adapt to the modern industrial era.

This is not the same as saying that the main impetus for change always comes from new ideas. Economic or political failures force change, and as institutions try to remain intact in the face of such pressure, they may themselves start to perform differently and inadvertently bring about significant change even as they maintain old external forms. Thus, for example, neither family structures nor the old religions from the agrarian past that have successfully survived behave exactly the way they did centuries ago. In the very act of conserving themselves, they have actually adapted and provoked further change.

Yet it remains true that it has to be from within abstractly generated ideas that plans for major social change or for new technologies have had to come. Thus the key question about social change is under what circumstances certain societies will offer a rich enough array of new possibilities to lead to adaptation when a crisis occurs.

We know that human societies try on the whole to restrain change. Sometimes they do this by deliberately persecuting new ideas. They are always inherently conservative unless dramatic evidence of failure makes them change. But why do some cultures come up with more innovative ideas than others and have them available when adaptation becomes necessary? Why were there so many original ideas floating around western Europe in the early modern period, and so few in the other agrarian civilizations of that time?

Though originally, at the start of the agrarian age, innovation—new technologies, new ways of administering society, new religions—almost all came from places with the highest population densities and thus the highest rate of exchange of ideas between individuals, this ceased to be the case later on. The oldest centers of agrarian civilization gradually became sclerotic and resistant to change, so that those on their margin contributed most important new ideas. This accounts for the astonishing originality of the ancient Greeks, or of the little city states in Italy during the Renaissance from the thirteenth to the sixteenth centuries, or of the Dutch merchant cities and England in the seventeenth and eighteenth centuries.

What about today? It has remained true in the twentieth century that somewhat marginal subgroups within the main industrial societies are the most innovative. In the United States, for example, scientific and economic advances have relied very heavily on immigrant groups, even though politics have by and large been controlled by older, better established elites. Religious dissenters or marginal foreign groups have played similar roles in most of the successful European societies as well, and in many parts of Africa, Latin America, and Asia.

This provides an essential clue about how likely it is that new ideas that eventually offer prospects for adaptive social change will occur. No culture that becomes too homogeneous, too self-satisfied, or too tied to old orthodoxies will produce enough new ideas. There is an analogy, though hardly a perfect one, in the biological world of evolution. If a species is reduced to too small a number, the gene pool becomes too small, and any minor crisis, such as a new disease or the presence of a maladaptive, mutated gene in one individual, can destroy the entire species. But if there is enough of a gene pool available, the possibility of evolving to meet such a crisis is much higher. As far as societies are concerned, then, the vitality and diversity of a culture and its resistance to uniformity now as always offer the best chances for successfully meeting future challenges.

The New or the Old?
The Paradox of Institutional Resistance to Change

In the past two centuries the pace of chance has accelerated so quickly that it sometimes seems that everything is different and that holding on to old forms of thought, action, or organization is certain to produce failure. But that is far from being the case, and successful social evolution does not imply that everything new is beneficial. On the contrary, drastic and rapid large-scale abandonment of old institutions or ways of thought is very unlikely to produce satisfactory results simply because there are too many untested elements in the new system, and some of these are bound to fail. The most extreme large-scale social experiments in the twentieth century took place in communist societies, whereas, quite paradoxically, the pace of institutional change in the more successful capitalist democracies was considerably slower and piecemeal.

This ought not be surprising. We have seen that a medieval institution, the English Parliament, turned out to be better adapted to handle the strains of rapid social change in the industrial revolution than the ostensibly more efficient and centralized bureaucracies of the absolutist monarchies of Europe. Similarly, many of the governing institutions in the United States are based on old English models, and in times of crisis they are accused of being hopelessly irrational and slow to respond. Yet it would be difficult to say that these outdated political bodies, originally designed to limit the power of government and divide it instead of concentrating it, have functioned poorly when compared to other types of political systems around the world. The more smoothly streamlined, centralized, and rationalized bureaucratic administrations in other societies have, on the contrary, led to many more serious failures than has the American system.

Another example of how institutional traditionalism, holding on to old patterns of organization, may be more adaptive than drastic innovation is family structure. The so-called "bourgeois" family of late nineteenth-century Europe was actually quite similar to the dominant type of family in agrarian Europe. The conjugal couple and their children were at its heart and provided mutual support for each other and their children. To be sure, there were many local variations and differences between the poor and the rich with respect to marriage and sexual behavior. But as societies became more urban and industrial, the small conjugal family as opposed to larger extended families of kinfolk became even more important than before, and other types of arrangements became less important. Yet the small conjugal family was far from being a purely modern invention. What emerged in bourgeois nineteenth-century Europe was not a drastic departure from much older patterns that had been a principal if not the exclusive mode of family life in preindustrial Europe. And in the late twentieth century it has been found that this type of family is still the most functional, that is, the most suitable for success-fully raising children and keeping the society working properly.

The anthropologist Jack Goody has found that when European and Asian family structures are compared, there were always more similari-ties than was once assumed. The conjugal, small family always played an important role in agrarian Asian civilizations, though in Asia also there were variations between regions, between different strata, and over time. With the advent of modernity, it is precisely the element of traditional family structure that emphasizes conjugal family ties that has become more important in the most successful Asian societies. In fact, in the East Asian societies of the late twentieth century, family patterns more closely resemble those of Victorian "bourgeois" Europe than the considerably looser and more fragile marriage ties which now exist in the West itself. That may be one reason why East Asian societies are economically more dynamic than the previously dominant West.

These two examples—the survival of old parliamentary forms that proved more adaptable in the modern world than more centralized and rationalized types of government, and the success of a particular type of family structure that turns out to be better adapted to the modern world than the more recent, more permissive types of arrangements that have grown in recent decades in the West—present us with a warning to be careful in evaluating social change. The new is not always better, and the plans thought up by social philosophers, ideologues, and other con-cerned intellectuals may act more like dysfunctional, harmful genes than like blueprints for a better society. Old social institutions that developed more or less on their own, that is, by the trial and error of dozens of generations rather than because of planned change or innovative ideals that stem from the conscious thinking of intellectuals, may, in some instances, work better than anything else.

And yet clearly innovation is sometimes necessary too, and the inhi-bition of change by old social institutions may occasionally prove cata-strophic. Also, new ideas consciously produced by intellectuals must sometimes play the key role. We saw that a social philosophy that legiti-mized capitalism was developed during the eighteenth century, and that this was an important element in making western Europe so econom-ically successful. Had older ideologies that condemned capitalist profits as evil and inferior to the search for honor and power prevailed, Europe might not have industrialized when it did. And it almost goes without saying that without the drive for greater scientific knowledge that char-acterized western European intellectual life from the Renaissance until the present, the transformations of the nineteenth and twentieth centuries would have been impossible.

There is absolutely no way of resolving this contradiction between the need to value institutional traditions worked out over long periods of time and the equally critical need to accept innovations and change other than through experimental trial and error. In the past as in the future, ideas for change will be tested by being carried out in some places, and economic or political success will tell us what works and what does not. We are probably no better at being able to judge ahead of time what will function than were our ancestors, though presumably we can gauge the results of any particular experiment more quickly than they did.

Freedom or Control?
The Dilemma of the Modern Era

Since at least the time of the invention of the state some five thousand years ago, people have faced a terrible dilemma. To give in to the state meant reducing individual freedom. But to resist the state meant, in the long run, weakening the ability of one's society to survive as a distinct and free entity. Over the thousands of years that agrarian states and civilizations dominated the world there seemed to be no solution to this dilemma, and most people simply became resigned to being unfree except in their dreams of a hoped-for afterlife. With the advent of the modern industrial age, the dilemma has returned because the enormous increase in material welfare combined with the spread of democratic ideals has made the ordinary individual far more autonomous than most peasants could ever be. It is now possible to envision a society that offers most of its members immense personal freedom: the freedom to choose how to live, where to live, and how to conduct their own personal relations. It is even possible for ordinary people to have some limited say in how the state itself will be run.

Greater individual freedom is not only desirable from the point of view of the individual who can enjoy it, but also likely to produce a more inventive, original society. This in turn will offer a society more alternatives from which to choose when it needs new solutions to social problems.

However, such freedom still poses the problem of how to maintain social cohesion. Not only do individuals need social support from units larger than their immediate families, but overly fragmented societies cannot finance the expensive educational, communications, legal, military, and many other needs without which the entire society would be gravely endangered. Furthermore, we know perfectly well that too much individual freedom can easily turn into an unrestrained search for rapid gratification that can make an entire society break down. This kind of general societal moral collapse was never possible in the past except for tiny, rich elites. But in the second half of the twentieth century it has become possible to foresee the possibility of such a disaster on a large scale in the wealthy industrial societies. It does not take much analytic power to see that certain parts of modern American society, for example, are losing all cohesion or moral restraint and that this tendency is increasing. What the consequences will be no one can foretell.

The late nineteenth-century German philosopher Friedrich Nietzsche expressed his loathing of capitalism's materialism, of political egalitarianism in democratic polities, and of cultural liberalism, all of which, he felt, were causing modern societies to degenerate. All segments of society did not have the potential to be creative or noble. Instead he wanted German society to be dominated by a hereditary, warrior aristocracy contemptuous of its inferiors. This was his way of resolving the dilemma of freedom and social control: Give freedom to a tiny, superior elite, and condemn most of corrupt humanity to the slavery it deserved. The elite, unlike the masses, would be able to discipline itself and not give in to crass, democratic materialism. But Nietzsche's vision, which was prescient in that it expressed much of the antidemocratic and anticapitalist sentiment of the twentieth century, leads to fascism. Giving the control of a modern society to a small elite that despises ordinary people and seeks glory over safe prosperity produces a militarized society devoted to war and the enslavement of those it conquers.

Karl Marx, who was equally contemptuous of capitalist, bourgeois society, and democracy, believed that all people had the capacity to be part of an idealized, self-regulated community where individual potential could be developed to the fullest without producing inequality or constraints of any kind. Marx's vision leads to communism. Not only is perfect equality impossible, but ordinary people, given a choice, prefer a modicum of prosperity and material satisfaction to pursuing impossible utopian dreams. Therefore it becomes necessary in a Marxist social system to impose the discipline and sacrifice necessary to bring about perfection. This leads to a form of oppression as great as that imposed by fascism.

The third alternative, to respect individual freedom and allow the market, that is the sum of individual wants and decisions, to determine the political and economic future of a society, has worked far better in the twentieth century than the major antimarket, elitist ideologies. In contrast to the case of the ancient conflict between state and prestate societies, so far there is no evidence at all that modern societies that diminish individual freedom in order to impose greater coordination actually succeed better. The broadly liberal vision of the eighteenth-century Enlightenment has proved to be stronger than the more recent views of the greatest nineteenth-century anticapitalist, antibourgeois thinkers.

Despite this record, it is not difficult to see why both Nietzschean and Marxist thought have appealed to those who want to overcome the moral flabbiness and political hesitancy of capitalist democracy. Such views have been especially attractive to twentieth-century intellectuals who naturally assume that they will be the elite in the more advanced societies of the future.

The industrial era is still young. Human societies are very far from having solved the ideological or economic problems of this era. There continue to be inequality, economic cycles of prosperity and decline, doubts about the morality of markets, confusion about the decline of communal solidarities, and a sense that with all our material success we should be able to obtain something finer than what we have. The tensions between greater freedom and the discipline that must be imposed by ruling elites in order to make complex societies work have never been resolved. The issue of industrial society's potential to degenerate into acquisitive, amoral anarchy is only now being faced. There is no guarantee at all that in the twenty-first century the old Enlightenment ideologies of the eighteenth century will continue to be the best guide to progress and a satisfactory future.

Studying the history of social change and understanding its general causes offers no answers to critical questions about the future. It does, however, make us more aware of the vast number of possible solutions that exist to social problems, and it teaches us to look at change in a very broad, comparative way. That is the only way to judge what works and what does not without having to wait for the cruel tests of physical extinction or for the violence and suffering experienced in the twentieth century before making up our minds.

Reference Notes
(Full references are in the bibliography)

Many of the works already cited contain essential aspects of the theoretical structure laid out in this chapter. Among the classical theorists,

Max Weber is the most important of those already mentioned. Though less historically informed, the theories of Emile Durkheim have been as influential as those of Weber. His book *The Division of Labor in Society* contains a whole theory about how societies become more differentiated as they progress and how this eventually leads to problems of social disorder that demand positive social policies to counteract them. Though Durkheim is easier to read than Weber, he also sounds more old-fashioned. Nevertheless, with some modifications, his theories are so widely believed by most American sociologists today that they are communicated through hundreds of secondary works that no longer even bother to cite him.

Friedrich Nietzsche was neither a social scientist nor a historian. He was a German philosopher who hated the modern world, especially conventional middle-class ideas, so much that he devoted his career to mocking them and proposing a different, bolder ethic. His ideas later became the basis for antimodernist philosophy and ideology that contributed to twentieth-century totalitarianism. With the seeming collapse of Marxism, Nietzschean thought is once again increasing its influence, particularly in much of the "postmodern" literary analysis in universities. This brilliant, outrageous, dangerous thinker can totally absorb even the most sophisticated reader. Sometimes Nietzsche is so witty while being right in his criticisms, and at other times he displays such erudition and implacable logic, that it is easy to overlook the consequences of his ideas. For those who really want to be challenged, I suggest picking up almost anything he wrote.

In the second half of the twentieth century there have been few if any social theorists who have matched Marx, Durkheim, or Weber in scope and in their ability to synthesize vast amounts of knowledge to explain how societies work. Talcott Parsons, whose career was in the middle third of the century, from the 1930s through the 1960s, is the one who comes closest. His massive tome *The Social System* can be hard to read, but it offers a comprehensive theory of society. The version of his theory that I have used is a further refinement of his thoughts. It was spelled out in considerable detail by Parsons and one of his best students, who is now an eminent senior sociologist at Berkeley, Neil Smelser, in their book *Economy and Society*.

The World in the Early Twentieth Century at the Height of European Imperialism

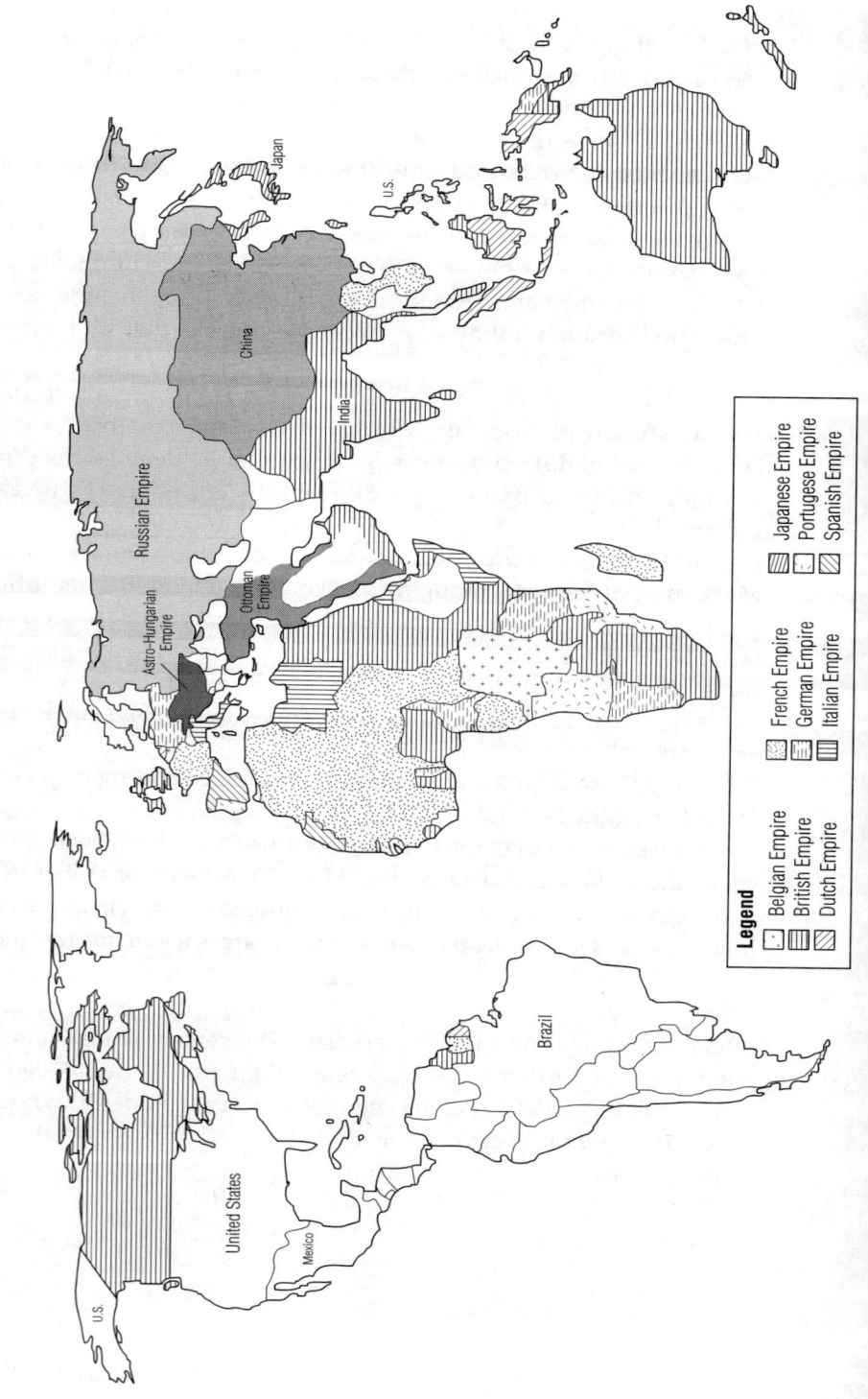

Japan

U.S.

China

Russian Empire

India

Astro-Hungarian Empire

Ottoman Empire

United States

U.S.

Mexico

Brazil

Legend

Belgian Empire	French Empire	Japanese Empire
British Empire	German Empire	Portugese Empire
Dutch Empire	Italian Empire	Spanish Empire

The World in the Late Twentieth Century:
The Rich, the Poor, and Those in the Middle

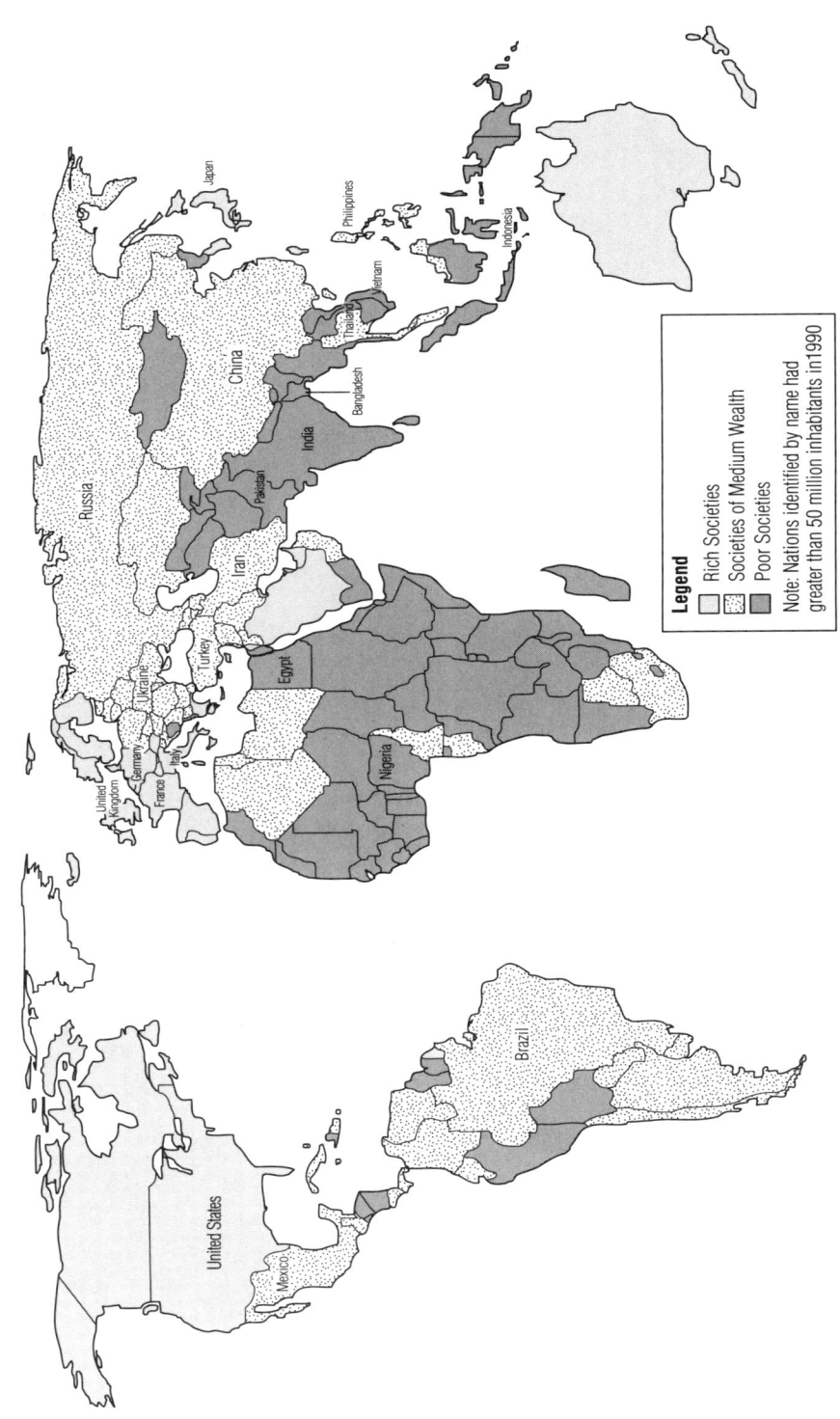

Legend

Rich Societies

Societies of Medium Wealth

Poor Societies

Note: Nations identified by name had greater than 50 million inhabitants in 1990

Bibliography

Except for a very small number of direct mentions of specific works and authors, there are no conventional footnote references in this text. The arguments are too general, and often too obviously summaries of very well-known positions taken by whole schools of social thought, to warrant a cumbersome scholarly apparatus. Nevertheless, I think it important to point out that the ideas I have expressed are summations of many other works. The ones listed below are those that I have already cited and also those I have found most useful over the past thirty years of reading and thinking about social change.

Anderson, Benedict R. *Imagined Communities: Reflections on the Origins and Spread of Nationalism*. London: Verso, 1983.

Baylin, Bernard. *The Ideological Origins of the American Revolution*. Cambridge, MA: Belknap Press of Harvard University, 1967.

Berlin, Isaiah. *Four Essays on Liberty*. London: Oxford University Press, 1969.

Bohannan, Paul. *Justice and Judgement among the Tiv*. London: Oxford University Press, 1957.

Bloch, Marc. *Feudal Society*. Chicago: University of Chicago Press, 1961.

Bloch, Marc. *French Rural History*. Berkeley: University of California Press, 1966.

Boserup, Ester. *Population and Technological Change: A Study of Long-Term Trends*. Chicago: University of Chicago Press, 1981.

Chagnon, Napoleon. *Yanomamö: The Fierce People*. New York: Holt, Rinehart & Winston, 1968.

Chirot, Daniel. *Social Change in the Modern Era*. San Diego: Harcourt Brace Jovanovich, 1986.

Chirot, Daniel. *Modern Tyrants: The Power and Prevalence of Evil in Our Age*. New York: Free Press, 1994.

Cipolla, Carlo M. *Guns, Sails and Empires: Technological Innovation and the Early Phases of European Expansion 1400-1700*. New York: Minerva, 1965.

Cipolla, Carlo M., ed. *The Economic Decline of Empires*. London: Methuen, 1970.

Degler, Carl N. *In Search of Human Nature: The Decline and Revival of Darwinism in American Social Thought*. New York: Oxford University Press, 1991.

Dumont, Louis. *Homo Hierarchicus: The Caste System and Its Implications*. Chicago: University of Chicago Press, 1980.

Durkheim, Emile. *The Division of Labor in Society*. New York: Free Press of Glencoe, 1964.

Elvin, Mark. *The Pattern of the Chinese Past*. Stanford, CA: Stanford University Press, 1973.

Finley, Moses I., ed. *The Legacy of Greece: A New Appraisal*. Oxford, UK: Clarendon, 1981.

Fortes, M., and E. E. Evans-Pritchard, eds. *African Political Systems*. London: Oxford University Press, 1940.

Galbraith, John K. *The New Industrial State*. Boston: Houghton Mifflin, 1967.

Gellner, Ernest. *Nations and Nationalism*. Ithaca: Cornell University Press, 1983.

Goldschmidt, Walter. *Man's Way: A Preface to the Understanding of Human Societies*. New York: Holt, Rinehart & Winston, 1959.

Goldstone, Jack A. *Revolution and Rebellion in the Early Modern World*. Berkeley: University of California Press, 1991.

Goody, Jack. *The Oriental, the Ancient and the Primitive: Systems of Marriage and the Family in the Pre-Industrial Societies of Eurasia*. Cambridge, UK: Cambridge University Press, 1990.

Gould, Stephen J. *Hen's Teeth and Horse's Toes*. New York: Norton, 1983.

Greenfeld, Liah. *Nationalism: Five Roads to Modernity*. Cambridge, MA: Harvard University Press, 1992.

Harris, Marvin. *Cannibals and Kings: The Origins of Cultures*. New York: Random House, 1978.

Hirschman, Albert O. *The Passions and the Interests: Political Arguments for Capitalism before Its Triumph*. Princeton: Princeton University Press, 1967.

Hirschman, Albert O. *Exit, Voice, and Loyalty: Responses to Decline in Firms, Organizations, and States*. Cambridge, MA: Harvard University Press, 1970.

Hobsbawm, Eric J. *The Age of Revolution 1789-1848*. New York: Mentor, 1962.

Hobsbawm, Eric J. *The Age of Capital 1848-1875*. New York: Scribner, 1975.

Hobsbawm, Eric J. *The Age of Empire 1875-1914*. New York: Pantheon, 1987.

Hodgson, Marshall G. *The Venture of Islam*. 3 vols. Chicago: University of Chicago Press, 1974.

Hosking, Geoffrey. *The Awakening of the Soviet Union*. Cambridge, MA: Harvard University Press, 1989.

Hughes, H. Stuart. *Consciousness and Society: The Reorientation of European Social Thought, 1890-1935*. New York: Knopf, 1958.

Johnson, Chalmers. *MITI and the Japanese Miracle: The Growth of Industrial Policy*. Stanford, CA: Stanford University Press, 1982.

Jones, Eric L. *The European Miracle*. Cambridge, UK: Cambridge University Press, 1981.

Jowitt, Kenneth. *The Leninist Response to National Dependency*. Berkeley: Institute of International Studies, 1978.

Katzenstein, Peter J. *Corporatism and Change: Austria, Switzerland, and the Politics of Industry*. Ithaca: Cornell University Press, 1984.

Kaye, Howard L. *The Social Meaning of Modern Biology: From Social Darwinism to Sociobiology*. New Haven: Yale University Press, 1986.

Kennedy, Paul M. *The Rise and Fall of Great Powers: Economic Change and Military Conflict from 1500 to 2000*. New York: Random House, 1987.

Kindleberger, Charles P. *The World in Depression*. London: Allen Lane, 1973.

Landes, David S. *The Unbound Prometheus: Technological Change and Industrial Development in Western Europe from 1750 to the Present*. Cambridge, UK: Cambridge University Press, 1969.

Leach, Edmund R. *The Political Systems of Highland Burma*. Boston: Beacon, 1965.

Lévi-Strauss, Claude. *The Elementary Structures of Kinship*. Boston: Beacon, 1969.

Malinowski, Bronislaw. *Magic, Science and Religion and Other Essays*. Garden City: Doubleday, 1954.

Mann, Michael. *The Sources of Social Power*. Vol. 1. Cambridge, UK: Cambridge University Press, 1986.

Marx, Karl. *Capital*. Vol. 1, *A Critical Analysis of Capitalist Production*. Edited by Frederick Engels. New York: International Publishers, 1967.

Marx, Karl. *Early Writings*. Introduced by Lucio Colletti. Harmondsworth, UK: Penguin, 1975.

Matthiessen, Peter. *Under the Mountain Wall: A Chronicle of Two Seasons in the Stone Age*. New York: Ballantine, 1962.

McEvedy, Colin. *The Penguin Atlas of Ancient History*. Harmondsworth, UK: Penguin, 1967.

McEvedy, Colin, and Richard Jones. *Atlas of World Population History*. Harmondsworth, UK: Penguin, 1978.

McNeill, William H. *Plagues and People*. Garden City, NY: Doubleday, 1976.

McNeill, William H. *The Pursuit of Power*. Chicago: University of Chicago Press, 1982.

Merton, Robert K. *Social Theory and Social Structure*. Glencoe, IL: Free Press, 1949.

Moore, Barrington, Jr. *The Social Origins of Dictatorship and Democracy: Lord and Peasant in the Making of the Modern World*. Boston: Beacon, 1967.

Nietzsche, Friedrich. *The Philosophy of Nietzsche*. New York: Random House, 1954.

North, Douglass C., and Robert Thomas. *The Rise of the Western World: A New Economic History*. Cambridge, UK: Cambridge University Press, 1971.

Olson, Mancur. *The Rise and Decline of Nations*. New Haven: Yale University Press, 1982.

Parsons, Talcott. *The Social System*. Glencoe, IL: Free Press, 1951.

Parsons, Talcott, and Neil J. Smelser. *Economy and Society: A Study in the Integration of Economic and Social Theory*. Glencoe, IL: Free Press, 1956.

Polanyi, Karl. *The Great Transformation*. Boston: Beacon, 1957.

Rogger, Hans, and Eugen Weber, eds. *The European Right: A Historical Profile*. Berkeley: University of California Press, 1966.

Rostow, Walt W. *The World Economy: History and Prospect*. Austin: University of Texas Press, 1980.

Schapiro, Leonard. *Russian Studies*. New York: Viking, 1987.

Schumpeter, Joseph A. *The Economics and Sociology of Capitalism*. Edited by Richard Swedberg. Princeton: Princeton University Press, 1991.

Scott, James C. *The Moral Economy of the Peasant: Rebellion and Subsistence in Southeast Asia*. New Haven: Yale University Press, 1976.

Service, Elman R. *Origins of the State and Civilization: The Process of Cultural Evolution*. New York: Norton, 1975.

Spence, Jonathan D. *The Search for Modern China*. New York: Norton, 1990.

Spooner, Brian, ed. *Population Growth: Anthropological Implications*. Cambridge: M.I.T. Press, 1972.

Trigger, B. G., B. J. Kemp, D. O'Connor, and A. B. Lloyd. *Ancient Egypt: A Social History*. Cambridge, UK: Cambridge University Press, 1983.

Vogel, Ezra P. *The Four Little Dragons: The Spread of Industrialization in East Asia*. Cambridge, MA: Harvard University Press, 1991.

Wakeman, Frederic, Jr. *The Fall of Imperial China*. New York: Free Press, 1975.

Weber, Max. *Economy and Society: An Outline of Interpretive Sociology*. Edited by Guenther Roth and Claus Wittich. New York: Bedminster, 1968.

Wolf, Eric. *Europe and the People without History*. Berkeley: University of California Press, 1982.

World Bank. *World Development Report*. New York: Oxford University Press, published annually.

Index